Ex Líbrís

Randy Manning

© APCo

HANGING
BASKETS

❖

DAVID SQUIRE

POCKET

GARDENING
GUIDES

HANGING
BASKETS

❖

DAVID SQUIRE

Illustrated by Vana Haggerty

Colour Library Books

Designed and conceived by

THE BRIDGEWATER BOOK COMPANY LTD

Art Directed by PETER BRIDGEWATER

Designed by TERRY JEAVONS

Illustrated by VANA HAGGERTY FLS

Edited by MARGOT RICHARDSON

CLB 3374

This edition published in 1994 by

Colour Library Books

© 1994 Colour Library Books Ltd

Godalming Surrey, England

Printed and bound in Singapore

ISBN 1-85833-152-8

CONTENTS

FROM VASE TO BASKET

FROM early times, in Mediterranean countries, plants have been grown outdoors in earthenware pots at ground level, or secured in pot-holders to walls. Small pots are still used in these ways and are especially attractive when grouped together on a wall, with other potted plants around them. Several modern variations of these pots are illustrated on pages 56 and 57.

MORE COMPOST NEEDED

The disadvantage of earthenware pots secured to walls is that they hold relatively little compost, and therefore their display is restricted to plants such as geraniums that have a slightly succulent nature. To create dominant, flower-packed displays, hanging baskets outdoors require more compost, and especially the ability to retain moisture. Wire-framed hanging baskets – traditionally lined with some sphagnum moss – admirably pro-vide these essentials.

Wall baskets are a direct development from animal mangers, although smaller.

MANY *American indoor hanging baskets were ornate and lavishly decorated. They were recommended for rooms, windows and piazzas, which suggests their design and use was strongly influenced by the many Italians who migrated to North America.*

FEW *Victorian houses were without plants, while many had lavish combinations of hanging potted plants and indoor fountains. These were often provided by professional gardeners.*

VICTORIAN VARIATION

Although ready-made indoor hanging baskets were widely available during the Victorian era, there was the opportunity to make your own, especially in rural areas. One of these ways was to hollow out the base of a large turnip and, in late summer or early autumn, to place a good-sized hyacinth bulb in it. It was essential to pack moss around the bulb, both to hold it secure and to help in the retention of moisture.

It was initially placed in a cool position but later, after roots had formed, taken into gentle warmth. At this stage, the turnip would develop fresh shoots that eventually curled around the bulb and created a highly decorative feature.

INDOOR *hanging baskets are more ornate than outside ones and are often supported with macramé frameworks. Nowadays, most indoor types are made of plastic, with an integral drip tray built into their base.*

TRADITIONAL *outdoor hanging baskets have a large, cup-shaped, wire-netting framework. This is hung from wires or chains attached to a metal wall-bracket. Some baskets are now made of plastic.*

WALL *baskets and mangers are secured to walls, then packed with plants. The basket types are smaller than the mangers and therefore require less compost and fewer plants to create a good display.*

AMERICAN CHOICES

In North America, indoor hanging baskets were originally known as hanging vases and, in the mid-1800s, considered an essential part of home decoration. Plants that trailed and created a graceful appearance were selected, but it was stressed that they had to be sufficiently vigorous to cover the container's sides with ornamental leaves and flowers.

Small-leaved ivies were popular, as they survived the heat from fires better than most plants. American books of that time offer a wide range of other plants for growing indoors, including petunias, *Torenia asiatica* (Wishbone Flower), mesembryanthemums (Icicle Plant), *Pentas carnea* (now *P. lanceolata* and known as Egyptian Star-cluster), Heliotrope (Turnsole and Cherry-pie), Verbena (Vervain), lycopodium (Clubmoss), tropaeolums (Nasturtium) and hoyas (Wax Vine and Porcelain Flower).

STREET DECORATION

Outdoor hanging baskets have increasingly been used to decorate streets in summer. Lamp posts are ideal supports, but because the baskets are fully exposed to drying winds and strong sunlight they often need to be watered several times a day at the peak of summer.

Because the cost of maintaining these baskets is high, they are frequently planted with foliage plants that are able to survive dry soil. Cascading, silver-leaved plants, such as the Licorice Plant (widely sold as Helichrysum petiolatum *but also known as* H. petiolare*) are especially suitable.*

DESIGN FACTORS

❖

HANGING baskets are superb for providing splashes of colour against walls, as well as brightening carports, porches, lobbies, verandahs, courtyards, terraces and roof gardens. They also introduce further summer colour and decoration when hanging from pergolas.

In warm climates it is possible to grow plants in baskets during winter, but in temperate regions the relatively small amount of compost in them is likely to freeze during wet and cold winters. Therefore, hanging baskets are best used in summer, from after the last frosts in spring to the onset of early ones in autumn. They can, however, be planted several weeks earlier and placed in a frost-proof greenhouse

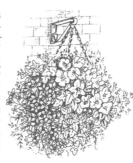

FEW *garden features are as attractive as hanging baskets. They create strong bursts of colour and provide further opportunities to grow plants, especially in small gardens.*

or conservatory until it is safe for them to be put outdoors. Indeed, this is the best way to grow them, as from the moment they are put outside they create dominant displays.

Trailing plants can also be grown indoors in hanging baskets, either with their pots removed and planted into compost, or just placed in a plastic basket. Planting indoor hanging baskets is described and illustrated on pages 18 and 19.

Unless a basket has a complete, non-drip base, it is essential that indoor types have drip-trays built into their bases to prevent carpets and furniture being damaged by water. Several designs of these baskets are available.

WINDOWS *frequently look dull and uninspiring. They can, however, be brightened throughout summer by positioning similarly sized hanging baskets on either side of them. Also, position wall baskets under windows.*

VERANDAHS *create slightly weather-sheltered places for hanging baskets. They introduce colour as well as rounded and cascading shapes to the often dominant vertical and horizontal frameworks.*

COURTYARDS *are enclosed by walls and buildings which can be easily brightened by a few hanging baskets. Take care not to position them where they could be knocked, and do not place them too near corners.*

DESIGN POSSIBILITIES

No other plant container is as versatile as a hanging basket. They can be positioned to highlight garden features, as well as to cloak others, and can be located wherever a firm fixing is available. Here are a few ideas about their use:

• Position a couple of baskets either side of a front door, but take care to put them where they will not be knocked. When hanging them, allow for an expansion in their width by mid-summer. This can be up to double the basket's normal width.

• Secure baskets either side of a large window: ensure that each bracket is located so that cascading foliage appears to cut across the window's vertical edges. If the basket is positioned to leave space at the window's edges, the effect will appear unplanned, fragmented and yet unified.

• When secured to a white-washed courtyard wall, allow space around each basket, so that it appears to be framed by an

CREATE *dominant features by placing troughs, large pots and hanging baskets in groups. These look especially attractive when highlighting windows. However, take care that hanging baskets do not drip water on plants in tubs or troughs below them.*

VICTORIANA

Ornate Victorian plant stands were often complex, forming ideal places for trailing plants in small plant holders, as well as ferns in pots. Small, cone-shaped containers were used to hold arrangements of cut flowers and ornamental foliage.

---

unending background. If hanging-baskets are hung so that their foliage overlaps each other, the area's size appears to be dramatically diminished.

• Never position a basket close to the corner of a building, as it may be knocked. Also, if it is too near a corner it appears to be an afterthought and not associated with the overall design. It is also likely to be buffeted by wind.

• To prevent passers-by knocking their heads or shoulders on hanging baskets, put a planted tub underneath, but not where water from the basket will drip on plants.

• Carports are quickly given a more exciting and colourful appearance by positioning a couple of hanging baskets on either side. Choose plants with either white flowers or silver leaves, so that they show up well at night. Avoid head-hitting positions.

• Camouflage unsightly drain-pipes with hanging baskets at head height, and clusters of tubs at ground level.

• In summer, lobbies and porches are ideal places for relatively hardy houseplants (see pages 44 to 49, and specific arrangements on

COLOUR HARMONIES AND BACKGROUNDS

❖

PLANTS in hanging baskets that colour co-ordinate with their backgrounds further enrich gardens and add a new dimension to gardening. This is especially important in small gardens, where it is essential to get the best from the space throughout the year. Here are suggested colours that harmonize with three differently coloured backgrounds – white, grey and red-brick walls. Clearly, colour is a matter of personal choice, but these suggestions offer basic guide-lines.

Many plants that are suitable for hanging baskets – such as lobelia, alyssum and petunias – have varieties in several colours. It is therefore essential to ensure the right ones are chosen. Many plants are suggested here, but they are not the only possibilities.

OTHER PLANTS FOR WHITE WALLS

- Asarina *'Victoria Falls'*: Cerise-purple trumpets about 5cm/2in long, borne in a tumbling mass from early summer to the frosts of autumn.
- Anagalis linifolia *'Gentian Blue'*: Masses of beautiful bright blue flowers from early to late summer.
- Nemophila menziesii *'Pennie Black'*: Deep purple to black flowers, with scalloped edges, from early to late summer.
- Geranium *'Classic Scarlet'*: A seed-raised geranium, with large, crimson-red flowers throughout summer. It creates a dominant display.

WHITE *walls form a bright background for plants. Plants with yellow, gold, scarlet or green flowers associate well with this backdrop, as do green leaves.*

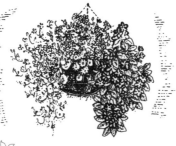

FLOWERS *in these colours can be planted on their own or in combinations with other suitable plants. Many plants have suitable varieties that are ideal for planting in hanging baskets.*

Lobelia erinus
(use blue varieties)

Brachycome iberidifolia
'Purple Splendour'

Impatiens
'Mega Orange'

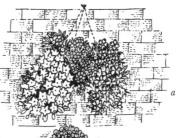

RED-BRICK *walls form dominant backgrounds for plants. Plants with white, soft blue, silver or lemon flowers form attractive constrasts. Also, use silver-leaved plants.*

BECAUSE *the wall's colour is strong, use dominant clusters of these colours so that they are easily noticeable, rather than a mass of mixed colours that remain insipid.*

Campanula carpatica *'Bellissimo'*

Alyssum maritimum (Lobularia maritima)

Nemophila maculata *'5-Spot'*

GREY-STONE WALLS

These create softer-coloured settings than white backgrounds and when seen from a distance are not so dominant, fusing more easily into the landscape. Harmonizing colours are deep purple, deep blue, pink and red.

- *Begonia pendula* 'Illumination Hybrid': Double, large flowers in shades of pink with cream centres.
- *Convolvulus tricolor* 'Rose Ensign': Trumpets up to 4cm/1¹/₂in wide, combining rose, lemon, pink and white, from mid to late summer.
- *Impatiens* 'Picotee Swirl': Compact plants bearing flowers with pink edges to each petal on a white to soft rose background.
- *Petunia* 'Celebrity Pink Morn': Beautiful pink flowers in summer.
- *Silene pendula* 'Peach Blossom': Cascading, with masses of frilly edged, 18mm/³/₄in-wide double flowers with deep pink buds changing to salmon and then white, from early to late summer.

OTHER PLANTS FOR RED-BRICK WALLS

- Brachycome iberidifolia *'White Splendour': Masses of white, daisy-like flowers from early to late summer.*
- Helichrysum petiolatum (H. petiolare): *Cascading stems bearing silvery leaves.*
- Impatiens *'Bright Eye': Large, white flowers with dark eyes. There are many other impatiens that harmonize against red walls.*
- Lobelia erinus *'White Cascade': The flowers swamp hanging baskets with masses of small flowers throughout summer. Light blue varieties also look good against red walls.*
- Petunia *'Super Cascade' (white forms): Ideal for hanging baskets, as it has a beautiful cascading nature.*

CHOOSING THE RIGHT PLANTS

❖

THE RANGE of plants that can be grown in hanging baskets is wide, and each year further ones are introduced by seed companies. However, they all have several things in common:

• They create a display of flowers or leaves from early to late summer. If plants are primarily grown for their flowers, new ones should appear regularly throughout summer. If plants are grown mainly for their leaves, these must remain attractive, even when old and at summer's end.

• They must be able to flourish in small amounts of compost and, preferably, not be invasive.

• They must respond to regular feeding from mid to late summer, which encourages the regular development of flowers.

• Preferably, plants should be in flower when planted in late spring or early summer.

• Choose plants that are not susceptible to pests and diseases. For example, although some Nasturtiums are ideal for planting in

hanging baskets, they attract blackfly, especially when grown in country areas with nearby crops of beans. For this reason, they are better grown in town gardens.

SINGLE-COLOUR THEMES

As well as creating medleys of colours and plants, it is equally exciting to plant hanging baskets with just one type of plant and in a single colour. There are many plants to choose from, including:

• <u>Balcon Geraniums:</u> These continental geraniums create masses of flowers, often in mixed colours but also available separately in scarlet, salmon and lilac.

• <u>*Calceolaria integrifolia (R. rugosa)* 'Sunshine':</u> Superb in a hanging basket, creating a feast of pouch-like, bright yellow flowers throughout summer.

• <u>*Campanula carpatica* 'Bellissimo':</u> Available in white or blue and creating a distinctive display of shallow bell-shaped flowers. It is ideal for growing in porches and lobbies, as well as outdoors.

SINGLE-COLOUR *baskets create dominant displays (page 13), but ensure they harmonize with the background colour (pages 10 and 11). Select plants that cascade and totally cloak baskets.*

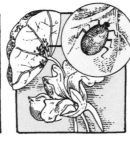

SOME *plants particularly attract pests: blackfly have a particular liking for Nasturtiums. In areas where these pests are a persistent problem, grow other plants. Greenfly is another major plant pest.*

IN MIXED *baskets combine foliage plants with flowers. Many foliage plants are better able to survive adverse conditions than flowering types, and therefore assure a long-lasting, bright display throughout summer.*

LOBBY BASKETS

Sheltered lobbies and porches create opportunities to protect baskets, normally hung outside, from buffeting wind and torrential rain. Additionally, trailing, relatively hardy indoor plants can be grown there during summer. A range of plants for lobbies and porches is recommended on pages 44 to 49, and plants that harmonize with each other are on pages 50 and 51. Always ensure that these plants are in drip-proof containers and cannot be knocked.

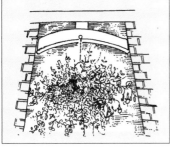

Indeed, it is a perennial and after flowering can be planted into a flower border.

- *Impatiens:* Several single-coloured forms with pendulous habits to choose from, including white, pastel pink, wine red, salmon, scarlet and lavender.
- Ivy-leaved Geraniums (Pelargoniums) have a straggly, rural appearance: choose plants of the same variety and position against a colour-harmonizing wall. The various colours include white, pink and red.
- *Lobelia erinus:* Choose trailing varieties, in colours including white, crimson, lilac and blue.
- *Mimulus* 'Malibu Orange': Beautiful orange flowers during summer. For a colour contrast, place a basket of this mimulus between two planted with *Mimulus* 'Malibu Mixed'.
- *Nierembergia* 'Mont Blanc': Creates masses of 2.5cm/1in-wide, cup-shaped, white flowers throughout summer. Position in full sun and regularly remove dead flowers to encourage the development of others.
- Petunias: There are many single-coloured, cascading forms well-suited for hanging baskets. Their colours include blue, ruby, white, pink, rose and salmon.

TOO *many different types of plants in a basket creates confusion and bewilders the eye. Therefore, select three types – a strong, dominant and cascading one for the centre and two trailers for the edges.*

TRY *colour variations within the same type of plant to reduce the risk of vigorous plants swamping their neighbours. This also creates a more evenly-shaped hanging basket than if different ones are used.*

DO NOT *pack too many plants into the same basket, as they will try to suffocate each other. Also, baskets that are too crowded tend to have a limited life, with the display becoming bare during mid-summer.*

BASKETS,
COMPOSTS AND LINERS

❖

HANGING baskets are unique containers and create unusual environments for plants. For that reason, care is essential when selecting the materials needed to create them.

• Baskets: There are three basic types: those with a plastic-coated wire framework; ones made of plastic with a drip-tray fitted into their bases; and large, bowl-shaped, plastic containers which have entire bases, without any provision for drainage or drip-trays underneath.

The wire type is ideal on patios, but where drips of water may spoil other plants or damage floors in lobbies and porches, the type with a drip-tray is best. Those without any drainage facility are used indoors, where plants are planted directly into them (see pages 18 and 19).

It is easier to create a dominant display in a large basket than in a small one. And the large one, when filled with compost, has the advantage of not drying out as rapidly. But always select a size of basket that harmonizes with its intended surroundings.

• Liners: Their purpose is to prevent compost falling through gaps in wire-framed baskets and to assist in the retention of moisture. Many are formed from recycled materials, and either moulded to the basket's shape or are flat and pre-cut so that they fit snugly.

Black plastic is frequently used as a liner. Although not aesthetically pleasing, it is soon covered with trailing stems. Dustbin liners or old plastic bags are inexpensive alternatives to consider.

Sphagnum moss has been the traditional liner for baskets, but it is costly and gathering it is not environmentally friendly. It is useful, however, for placing over the compost after planting, creating an attractive appearance and reducing moisture loss.

• Metal brackets: These are essential to support hanging baskets. Choose strong ones.

COMPOSTS FOR HANGING BASKETS

Compost is crucially important when growing plants in hanging baskets, where a plant's root growth is restricted to frameworks 25–50cm/10–20in wide and about half as deep.

Proprietary composts are widely available and some have extra materials in them that assist in moisture-retention. Some varieties also include slow-acting fertilizers.

It is possible to make your own compost, but if only a few baskets are to be planted it is much easier to buy it in bags, ready prepared.

Peat-based composts are better than loam-based types for hanging baskets, as they retain more moisture. To assist this, add moisture-retaining additives such as perlite and vermiculite to the compost.

In past years, shredded cork was frequently used to retain moisture in hanging baskets, as well as in windowboxes.

WIRE-FRAMED *hanging baskets are usually formed of plastic-covered wire, normally green but also black or white. Their sizes and shapes vary, from 25cm/10in to 50cm/20in wide.*

BASKETS *with drip-trays are ideal for use in lobbies and porches. Such containers help to conserve moisture in the compost.*

BRACKETS *to support hanging baskets must be strong and well secured to a wall. Most are coated in white, green or black plastic to enhance them and to increase their life expectancy. They are sold in several sizes (20–35cm/ 8–14in long) to suit the basket's width and to ensure it does not knock against the wall.*

ALL *liners have the same purpose: to conserve moisture in the compost. Some are cup-shaped and available in several sizes to fit all baskets. Some are formed of recycled paper.*

TO ENSURE *they fit snugly into baskets, some liners, although bought flat, fit snugly into a basket's base.*

MANY *liners are formed of environmentally friendly materials, including coir matting.*

BLACK *polythene is widely used as a liner. Alternatively, use bin-liners.*

PLANTING A
WIRE-FRAMED BASKET

❖

PLANT hanging baskets in spring, using half-hardy annuals as well as foliage plants like the Licorice Plant (*Helichrysum petiolatum/ H. petiolare*) and tender perennials such as pelargoniums and cascading fuchsias.

INFLUENCE OF FROST

The precise time in spring when hanging baskets are planted depends on the weather. Some areas are frost free in early spring, while others still have frosts until early summer. However, it is possible to plant baskets before the risk of frost has passed, and instead of immediately placing them outdoors to put them temporarily in a frost-proof greenhouse or conservatory. This also gives plants a chance to become established and to create a display before being placed outdoors. However, while these baskets are waiting to be put outside, do not expose them to high temperatures. If possible, put the baskets outside

during the day and move them back into a greenhouse at night. Alternatively, open the door and ventilators fully during the day.

After hanging baskets are placed outdoors, low temperatures are sometimes forecast at night. Plants can be given slight protection by placing a couple of layers of newspaper over them. Wedging

1. PLACE *a wire-framed basket in the top of a bucket and line it with black polythene. Mould it to the basket's shape, then cut off 5cm/2in above the rim. The plastic may need further trimming later.*

2. PLACE *a handful of moist peat in the basket's base, then add and firm the compost to about half the container's depth. Take care not to push compost or your fingers through the plastic sheeting at the sides.*

3. MAKE *5cm/2in-long slits in the polythene, at about 10cm/4in apart and level with the surface of the compost. Push the roots of trailing plants through each hole, then cover and firm them with compost.*

the papers under the supporting chains is usually quite sufficient to hold them in position, as at that time of year the frost risk is from clear skies, rather than cold, searing winds.

CAREFUL WATERING

After initially watering the compost, take care during the following three or four weeks not to excessively moisten the compost, as this could keep it unnecessarily wet and cold, delaying establishment and encouraging roots to decay. However, once the plants are growing strongly and their roots are spread throughout the compost, more water is needed. Always apply water gently, as until roots fill the surface compost there is a risk of it being disturbed and washed about by forceful jets of water.

INITIAL STOPPING

A few young plants, such as fuchsias and foliage plants, need stopping (removal of shoot tips) to encourage them to develop sideshoots and become bushy. Pinch back the shoots to just

HANGING IN A GREENHOUSE

Place newly-planted hanging baskets in frost-proof greenhouses or conservatories to enable rapid establishment. Do not place them outside until all risk of severe frosts has passed, and keep the compost moist during this period.

Strong hook

above a pair of leaves. Place the removed shoot tips on a compost heap: do not leave them in the basket as this could encourage the onset of diseases. It is also unsightly. Removing the soft tips of shoots also makes plants less attractive to greenfly.

. ADD *more compost and plant a dominant, cascading plant in the centre. The surface of its soil-ball should be 12–18mm/^{1}/2–^{3}/4in below the basket's rim. Add trailing plants around it, over and firm with compost.*

5. WHEN *the planting is complete, the compost's surface should be 12mm/^{1}/2in below the basket's rim. This enables the compost to be watered. Place a thick layer of sphagnum moss over the surface and rim.*

6. LEAVE *the basket in a bucket and gently water the compost twice so that it settles around the roots of plants. When excess water has drained, suspend the basket in a greenhouse until it is established.*

PLANTING
INDOOR HANGING BASKETS

❖

DISPLAYING houseplants in hanging baskets introduces a new dimension to indoor gardening. There are two basic ways to achieve this: taking the plants out of their pots and planting them into compost in a container, or leaving them in their pots and standing them in a flat-based, plastic hanging basket.

Clearly, wire-framed, outdoor-type hanging baskets are not suitable for use indoors, as water would drip over carpets. Instead, plastic types with drip-trays built into them are used when plants are left in their pots. They can also be used where plants are removed from their

INDOOR *hanging baskets introduce eye-height colour. When used in conjunction with troughs, they create attractive room dividers. Alternatively, suspend them over a coffee table, where they cannot be knocked.*

containers, although if plants are watered carefully, containers with neither drainage holes nor drip-trays can be used.

The main advantage of leaving plants in their pots and just placing them in a basket, is that as plants cease flowering they can be replaced. Also, invasive types can be removed without radically affecting other plants. It is, however, slightly more difficult to water them, as each plant must be attended to separately, unlike the other method when all the plants are in the same compost. For either method, if the position is shaded, use foliage plants rather than flowering plants.

1. ONE *way to grow plants in hanging baskets indoors is to remove their pots and plant them directly into a container. First, cut a piece of paper to the size and shape of the basket's base, and arrange the plants attractively on it.*

2. POSITION *a container in the top of a plastic bucket, to hold it firm. Fill the container's base with 18mm/3/4in of shingle, then a layer of peat-based potting compost, so that its surface is about 15cm/6in below the container's rim.*

3. SET *the plants in the container, using the same arrangement as shown in step one. Remove the pots, position the plants and pack compost around them. Ensure the surface of each root-ball is 12–18mm/ 1/2–3/4in below the rim.*

1. HOUSEPLANTS *can be left in their pots and displayed in a flat-based hanging basket fitted with a drip-tray. Pre-arrange the plants on a sheet of paper, then form a 2.5cm/1in-thick layer of pea-shingle in the basket's base.*

2. WATER *the plants a few hours before arranging them. Fill the container with plants, starting from the centre and working towards the outside. Position plants with their attractive 'face' sides pointing towards the basket's outside.*

3. TO REDUCE *the amount of watering needed, pack moist peat between the pots. This also helps to keep the compost cool. Do not cover the compost, as each pot must be watered individually, according to the dryness of the compost.*

FOLIAGE PLANTS FOR INDOOR HANGING BASKETS

- Devil's Ivy (*Epipremnum pinnatum/Scindapsus aureus*): Trailing stems bearing shiny green leaves blotched in yellow.
- Emerald Fern (*Asparagus densiflorus* 'Sprengeri'): Arching, wiry stems packed with long, needle-like leaves.
- Mother of Thousands (*Saxifraga stolonifera* 'Tricolor'): Roundish to heart-shaped, green leaves edged in white and pink, and long, wiry stems often 60cm/2ft or more long, bearing small plantlets.
- Spider Plant (*Chlorophytum comosum* 'Variegatum'): Long, tapering, cascading, green and white leaves. Eventually, it can form a plant more than 90cm/3ft across.
- Swedish Ivy (*Plectranthus coleoides* 'Marginatus'): Attractive light green leaves with scalloped edges about 5cm/2in wide that reveal broad, white edges.
- Swedish Ivy (*Plectranthus oertendahlii*): Trailing stems with 2.5cm/1in-wide, slightly heart-shaped, green leaves with prominent veins.

FLOWERING PLANTS FOR INDOOR HANGING BASKETS

- Basket Begonia (*Begonia* x *tuberhybrida* 'Pendula'): Wide colour range of pendulous flowers borne in clusters during summer. Single and double-flowered forms.
- Flame Flower (*Episcia cupreata*): Trailing stems bearing oval, 5–7.5cm/2–3in-long, dark green leaves with silver or pale green veins. During summer it develops tubular, orange-red flowers with yellow eyes.
- Goldfish Plant (*Columnea gloriosa*): Trailing stems up to 90cm/3ft long, packed with small leaves and tubular, 7.5cm/3in-long scarlet and yellow flowers from late autumn to spring. Requires high temperatures in winter.
- Italian Bellflower (*Campanula isophylla*): Easily grown, with blue, star-shaped flowers from mid-summer to early autumn. There also is a white-flowered form.
- Lady's Eardrops (*Fuchsias*): There are many slightly tender, trailing fuchsias that can be grown in indoor hanging baskets. Ensure the compost does not become dry.

SECURING A BASKET

❖

FEW gardening sights are more sobering and regrettable than a hanging basket that has fallen from a broken bracket and burst apart on the ground. And except for the devastation caused by freak summer storms, such catastrophes are usually avoidable.

DANGER POINTS

There are always weak and vulnerable points in the construction of anything, and here are a few to be aware of when securing hanging baskets:

• Always use proper masonry fixings when securing brackets to walls; never knock matchsticks into holes instead of sound fixings. And ensure the drill size is compatible with the fixing; builders' merchants and hardware shops will always advise on this.

• Do not reuse corroded brackets stored from several years earlier.

• Do not reuse partly corroded screws, as they may break and the bracket collapse. Also, if their heads snap off it is difficult to remove them from the wall.

SECURING TO BARGE-BOARDS

In bungalows where the eaves extend about 38cm/15in beyond the brickwork, it is possible to screw strong cup-hooks into the barge-board. However, this can only be done if the barge-board is made of wood, rather than plastic. Never underestimate the weight of a basket when watered: buy the strongest fixing possible.

• Always check chains used to secure hanging baskets to their brackets. Replacement chains are available to suit baskets from 25cm/10in wide to 50cm/20in wide. If chains that are too small are used, it puts unnecessary strain on both the basket and the chain, causing them to warp and break.

WHEN *fitting a wall-bracket, hold it upright and in position, then use a pencil to mark the wall with the positions of the securing holes. If the bracket is at an angle, the weight of the basket may eventually twist it off the wall.*

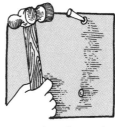

DRILL *the wall – ensuring it is sound and firm – and use masonry fixings to plug it. The size of the drill must enable the fixing to fit snugly; it usually needs a few light taps of a hammer to make it flush with the wall's surface.*

USE *galvanized screws that are long enough to pass through the holes in the bracket and to the depths of the holes. First, partly turn both screws into the wall, then tighten. Do not screw one in fully before attending to the other one.*

WATERING HANGING BASKETS

❖

NO OTHER plant containers are as exposed to drying sun and winds way as hanging baskets. It therefore is not surprising that they need special attention and watering several times a day during the height of summer. Apart from watering the baskets in the ways illustrated, there are a few others to consider, which can reduce the frequency of watering:

• Proprietary hose-pipe fittings and trigger mechanisms enable the baskets to be watered from ground level.

• On exceptionally hot days, dampen the wall and patio area around baskets. This is because hot walls reflect heat and speed up the drying process.

• Mix water-retentive additives, such as vermiculite and perlite, to composts (see pages 14 and 15).

• If water runs out of the compost, leave it for half an hour and then water again. The first watering will expand the compost, the second one will saturate it.

• If the basket is large, put a plastic saucer in its base while planting it. This acts as a reservoir, full of moist compost.

• During very hot days, drop a few ice-cubes on top of the compost. These eventually melt and provide extra water.

IMMERSING IN A BOWL

Peat-based composts that become dry are difficult to re-moisten. If this happens, take down the basket and immerse the complete compost area in a bowl of water until bubbles cease to rise. Allow to drain before replacing on a bracket.

WATERING *hanging baskets is not easy: one way is to stand on a stool and use a watering-can. This is very difficult, as well as perilous. However, filling the can only half full makes the task easier. Remove the rose from the can.*

TYING *the end of a hose-pipe to a 1.2m/4ft-long cane makes watering easier. Raise the can and gently trickle water on the compost until it spills over the edge. Bend the top of the hose over to prevent water running back down it and up your sleeves.*

HANGING *baskets suspended too high to be watered from step-ladders are best fitted with pulleys so that they can be lowered. Ensure the pulley mechanism is safe and the basket will not fall. Also, beware of water dripping on passers-by.*

KEEPING PLANTS HEALTHY

❖

WATERING and feeding are the main precautionary measures for keeping plants healthy. If these are neglected, their display is limited and may end six or so weeks earlier than it should. If you have any doubts about being able to feed the plants regularly, add slow-release fertilizers to the compost when planting the basket. Water the plants every ten days with a general plant fertilizer as well. Prepare the mixture exactly to the manufacturer's instructions, as if it is too strong it may damage plants.

CONTROLLING
PESTS AND DISEASES

Before placing hanging baskets outdoors, spray them thoroughly with a general insecticide. Then check them every week, looking both on top and under leaves.

As a precautionary measure – and especially where containers are difficult to reach and inspect – insert insecticide pins into the compost. These are like small cardboard sticks, and release an insecticide that is absorbed by the roots to protect the entire plant. Such insecticides are known as systemic, as chemicals spread within plants and kill insects that suck their sap.

Unlike most plants, even those in tubs, pots and urns, hanging baskets are free from slugs and snails, which during warm and moist summer evenings can devas-

---

PESTS AND DISEASES

Because the plants are packed close together, they provide concentrated meals for pests. Inspect plants regularly and as soon as pests or diseases are noticed, spray with an insecticide or fungicide. Use environmentally friendly sprays that will not harm the atmosphere.

REGULARLY *pinch off dead or faded flowers from plants to induce the development of further blooms. If left on plants they encourage the presence of diseases, as well as spoiling the display's appearance.*

FEED *plants regularly throughout summer, using a fertilizer dissolved in water. Apply this every ten to fourteen days. First, however, water the compost: never apply fertilizer to dry compost – it damages roots.*

REGULARLY *nip out the growing points of young plants to encourage bushiness. Fuchsias especial[ly] need encouragement to develop sideshoots, and the tips of their shoots need to be nipped out often.*

HANGING BASKETS

ate plants overnight. However, plants in wall baskets and mangers are not so fortunate and therefore it is necessary to use baits. Place them under tiles or raised pots on the ground around the basket's base. This prevents the bait becoming wet and reduces the risk of inquisitive pets and young children sampling them. Once the bait becomes wet, remove it and replace with fresh pellets. If left, it encourages the development of harmful moulds.

STORM AND WIND DAMAGE

Mid-summer storms sometimes flatten plants in hanging baskets, especially when in exposed positions. Nothing can be done during a storm – except taking them down and putting in a greenhouse or conservatory – but afterwards cut off damaged flowers and broken stems. Initially, this action may appear to be drastic, but if a tangle of stems and bruised flowers remains it encourages the presence of diseases, especially if the weather remains damp and warm. Feeding also aids quick recovery.

Should storms occur early in summer, it is better to replace damaged plants with healthy ones.

BUYING GUIDE

Don't buy plants that are:
* *thin and weak – they will never recover.*
* *excessively large plants in small amounts of soil. This indicates that their roots are congested.*
* *small plants in large amounts of soil. Such plants may have only recently been pricked out into pots and their roots not established.*
* *infested with pests or diseases.*
* *growing in dry compost – it shows they have been neglected.*
* *that are not labelled. If later they prove not to be the variety you want, the entire colour scheme could be ruined.*

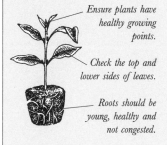

Ensure plants have healthy growing points.

Check the top and lower sides of leaves.

Roots should be young, healthy and not congested.

ITALIAN INFLUENCES

During the early part of the nineteenth century, Italian gardens were particularly noted for their romantic nature. They frequently had large, ornate pots and urns, which were a natural development from the Italian Renaissance. Many were positioned at the junctions of paths.

PLANTS FOR
HANGING BASKETS 1

❖

THE range of summer-flowering, half-hardy plants that can be grown in hanging-baskets is wide. They are also ideal for planting in wall baskets, where they help to cloak the sides with flowers. However, not all plants that are recommended for wall baskets and mangers can be planted in hanging baskets, as they are either too large or without a trailing or pendulous habit.

RAISING PLANTS

• <u>Floss Flower (*Ageratum houstonianum*):</u> Sow seeds 3mm/¹⁄₈in deep in early spring in 10–16°F/50–61°F. Germination takes ten to fourteen days. When the seedlings are large enough to handle, transfer them to seed-trays and later acclimatize to outdoor conditions.

PLANTING DISTANCE

Plants in hanging baskets are planted much closer together than when in a border in a garden, or even in tubs. This is because hanging baskets are relatively small and a colour-packed display is essential. In wall baskets and mangers, plants at the edges can be left slightly further apart because those in the centre are usually relatively large and dominant. Therefore, the spacings suggested from here and until page 36 may appear close, but create successful displays.

Regular attention is necessary to ensure pests and diseases do not manage to establish themselves in the display (see pages 22 and 23).

AGERATUM
HOUSTONIANUM *(Floss
Flower): Height 13–30cm/
5–12in, plant 13–15cm/
5–6in apart. Ideal when
forming a collar in large
hanging baskets or wall
baskets.* Clustered, powder-
puff-like blue, pink or white
flowers in summer.

ALYSSUM MARITIMUM
(now Lobularia
maritima): *Height 7.5–
15cm/3–6in, plant 15cm/
6in apart. Carpeting and
trailing, in white, rosy-red
and deep purple throughout
summer. Plant trailing types
of this plant around the
sides of baskets.*

ANAGALLIS LINIFOLIA
*'Gentian Blue' (Pimpernel):
Height 15–23cm/6–9in,
plant 13–15cm/5–6in
apart. Low growing and
sprawling, with masses of
12–18mm/¹⁄₂–³⁄₄in-wide
rich blue flowers with bright
coloured centres, from early
to late summer.*

SARINA PURPUSII
*Victoria Falls': Height
3–15cm/5–6in, plant
5–20cm/6–8in apart. It
creates a tumbling fountain
of cerise-purple, 5cm/2in-
ong trumpets from early
 summer to autumn. The
stems often trail for
8cm/15in.*

BEGONIA
SEMPERFLORENS *(Wax
Plant): Height 15–23cm/
6–9in, plant 15–20cm/
6–8in apart. Bushy,
floriferous plants, packed
with flowers from early to
late summer. Many attractive
colours, including white, pink
and scarlet.*

BEGONIA x
TUBERHYBRIDA
*'Pendula' (Basket Begonia):
Height 15–20cm/5–8in,
plant 25cm/10in apart.
Slender, trailing stems that
create a dominant feature in
hanging baskets. Colours
include red, yellow and pink,
from early to late summer.*

Sweet Alyssum (*Alyssum mariti-
um/Lobularia maritima*): Sow seeds
mm/¹/₄in deep during late win-
er and early spring in 10–13°C/
0–55°F. Germination takes seven
to ten days. Later, prick out the
seedlings into small clusters and
lowly acclimatize them to out-
oor temperatures.

Pimpernel (*Anagallis linifolia*):
ow seeds 3mm/¹/₈in deep in late
inter or early spring and place in
6°C/61°F. Germination takes
wo to three weeks. When the
seedlings are large enough to han-
le, transfer them to small pots or
eed-trays and slowly acclimatize
o outdoor conditions.

Asarina purpusii: Sow seeds on
he surface of compost during late
inter and early spring in 21–
4°C/70–75°F. Germination takes
wo to four weeks. When large
nough to handle, transfer the
eedlings into small pots or seed-
rays and slowly acclimatize to
utdoor conditions.

• Wax Plant (*Begonia semperflorens*):
Sow seeds thinly on the surface of
compost (do not cover) during late
winter and early spring. Water
lightly and place in 16–20°C/
61–68°F. Germination takes two
to four weeks. When large enough
to handle, prick off the seedlings
into small clusters and gradually
acclimatize them to outdoor conditions and temperarures.

• Basket Begonia (*Begonia x tuberhybrida* 'Pendula'): Plant tubers in
7.5–10cm/3–4in-deep boxes filled
with moist peat in early and mid-
spring and place in 18°C/64°F.
Keep moist and when shoots
develop transfer them singly into
pots of peat-based compost.
Reduce the temperature slightly,
keep moist and transfer to
10–13cm/4–5in-wide pots. Slowly
acclimatize to outdoor temperatures and plant into baskets. Do
not expose plants to low temperatures or draughts, as the buds
might then drop off.

PLANTS FOR
HANGING BASKETS 2

❖

HERE are many more plants to consider for planting in hanging baskets, wall baskets and mangers. Some of these form dominant centre-pieces in hanging baskets, while others are better for planting around the sides.

RAISING PLANTS

• Seed-raised Pendulous Begonias (*Begonia pendula* 'Illumination'): Sow seeds thinly on the surface of compost (do not cover) during early spring and place in 16–20°C/61–68°F. Germination takes two to four weeks. When large enough to handle, transfer the seedings into small pots and slowly acclimatize to outdoor conditions.

• Swan River Daisy (*Brachycome iberidifolia*): Sow seeds 3–6mm/ 1/8–1/4in deep during early and mid-spring in 18°C/64°F. Germination takes about ten days. When large enough to handle, transfer the seedlings into seed-trays or small pots and plant when all risk of frost has passed.

VICTORIAN
FLOWER BOWLS

During the 1840s, displaying flowers in suspended baskets became popular. In 1841, Mrs J. C. Loudon's The Ladies' Companion to the Flower Garden *tells that containers such as these were suspended in greenhouses and planted with 'the creeping Cereus, Moneywort, and other common plants which produced their flowers on hanging stems, as for Epiphytes and orchideous plants.'*

• Slipper Flower (*Calceolaria integrifolia* 'Sunshine': Sow seeds – jus pressing them into the surface during early spring in 15–20°C 59–68°C. Germination takes two

BEGONIA PENDULA *'Illumination': Height 15–20cm/6–8in, then trailing, plant 20cm/8in apart. Masses of large, double flowers in shades of pink, many with cream centres, throughout summer.*

BRACHYCOME IBERIDIFOLIA *'Splendour' (Swan River Daisy): Height 23–30cm/9–12in, plant 15–20cm/6–8in apart. Each plant produces masses of flowers in blue to purple or white in summer.*

CALCEOLARIA INTEGRIFOLIA *'Sunshine (Slipper Flower): Height 25–38cm/10–15in, plant as a centre-piece in a hanging basket, where it develops bright yellow, pouch-like flowers.*

CAMPANULA CARPATICA *'Bellissimo'*: *Height 15cm/6in, then trailing, plant about 20–23cm/8–9in apart. Masses of chalice-shaped, 5cm/2in-wide, blue or white flowers from early to late summer. Creates a massed display.*

CAMPANULA ISOPHYLLA *(Star of Bethlehem): Height 15cm/6in, then trailing, plant 20cm/8in apart. Masses of star-shaped, 2.5cm/1in-wide, blue flowers from mid to late summer. There is also a white form.*

CONVOLVULUS TRICOLOR *'Rose Ensign': Height: 10–15cm/4–6in, then trailing, plant 20–25cm/8–10in apart. Masses of beautiful, rose, lemon, pink and white, trumpet-like flowers from mid to late summer.*

to three weeks. When the seedlings are large enough to handle, transfer them into small pots, slowly harden off and plant into a hanging basket.

• *Campanula carpatica* 'Bellissimo': Sow seeds – just pressing them into the compost – in late winter and early spring. When the seedlings are large enough to handle, transfer them to seed-trays or small pots and slowly acclimatize to outdoor conditions.

• Star of Bethlehem (*Campanula isophylla* 'Krystal' varieties): Sow seeds 3mm/^{1}/8in deep in 16°C/61°F in late winter. Prick off the seedlings into seed-trays or small pots, slowly harden off and plant into containers when all risk of frost has passed. Before the introduction of 'Krystal' varieties, this species always had to be raised from cuttings.

• *Convolvulus tricolor* 'Rose Ensign': Sow seeds 3mm/^{1}/8in deep in 15–18°C/59–64°F during early spring. When the seedlings are large enough to handle, prick out into seed-trays and slowly accustom to outdoor conditions.

FUCHSIAS

❖

EW plants capture such attention and admiration as fuchsias. They are native mainly to Southern and Central America and in general are tender in temperate countries and thereby vulnerable to frosts. A few, such as *Fuchsia magellanica*, are relatively hardy, but those grown in hanging baskets are tender.

SUITABLE PLANTS

Although it is possible to raise your own fuchsias from cuttings, if only a few plants are needed it is much easier to order established plants from specialist nurseries, or to buy them from garden centres. Whatever the source, they cannot be planted outdoors until all risk of frost has passed. However, if a frost-proof greenhouse or conservatory is available, hanging baskets can be planted earlier and placed in them until outdoor conditions improve. Ensure these plants have had their shoot tips removed to encourage the development of sideshoots. Not all varieties are suitable for hanging baskets, but the following are superb.

FUCHSIAS FOR HANGING BASKETS

• 'Cascade': Single; white sepals flushed carmine, and deep red petals. Attractive drooping habit.
• 'Falling Stars': Single; pale scarlet sepals and turkey-red petals with slight orange tints.

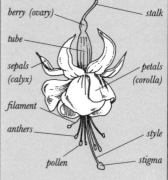

PARTS OF A FLOWER

Fuchsia flowers appear complex, but have the same basic parts as other flowers. Their intricate nature has made them widely known as Lady's Eardrops.

berry (ovary) — stalk
tube —
sepals (calyx) — petals (corolla)
filament —
anthers — style
pollen — stigma

WHEN *planting a basket totally with fuchsias, create a quick display by planting five or seven bushy and trailing plants of the same variety around the edges.*

WHEN *mixing fuchsias with other plants, plant a dominant, cascading variety in the centre. Put trailing plants around the edges to clothe the basket's sides.*

FUCHSIAS *are superb in hanging baskets, as their flowers can be readily seen at eye-height. It is essential, however, to choose cascading types (see above and right).*

SINGLE FLOWERS *are distinguished by having only four petals. They reveal a simple elegance. These include old varieties, such as 'Achievement', 'Brutus', 'Coachman', 'Dr. Foster' and 'Display'.*

SEMI-DOUBLE FLOWERS *have five, six or seven petals. These include 'Alice Hoffman', 'Lena', 'Muriel', 'Papoose', 'Phyllis', 'Pink Pearl', 'Snowcap', 'Trase', 'Walsingham' and 'Westminster Chimes'.*

DOUBLE-FLOWERS *have eight or more petals, and to many eyes appear too cluttered. Examples include 'Annabel', 'Constance', 'Dollar Princess', 'Harry Gray', 'Heidi Ann', 'Pink Galore' and 'Swingtime'.*

- '**Golden Marinka**': similar to 'Marinka', but with golden foliage.
- '**Harry Gray**': Double; white sepals, shading to rose-pink, and white petals shading to rose-pink.
- '**Jack Acland**': Single; bright pink tube and sepals, and deep rose petals.
- '**La Campanella**': Semi-double; white sepals flushed white, and imperial purple petals changing to a more suitable lavender.
- '**Lakeside**': Single; vigorous and branching variety with bluish-violet petals veined in bright pink. As the flowers mature, this fades to a shade of lilac.
- '**Lena**': Semi-double; very free-flowering, with rosy-magenta petals, flushed pink and paling at their bases. The flowers are medium sized.
- '**Marinka**': Single; rich red sepals, and dark red petals.
- '**Swingtime**': Double; rich, shiny red sepals and milky-white coloured petals.
- '**Walshingham**': Semi-double; off-white and rose-pink sepals, and pale-lilac petals.

NAUTICAL INTRODUCTION

The introduction of fuchsias from Southern and Central America into England is uncertain, but one story tells how, in the 1790s, James Lee, the owner of the famous Vineyard Nursery in London, saw a fuchsia growing in the window of a cottage in Wapping. It was said to have been brought from South America by a sailor and given to his mother. Stories suggest that Lee paid eighty guineas for it. It is more likely that Lee got the plants from Kew Gardens, donated by Captain Firth on return from South America.

Fuchsia macrantha

PLANTS FOR
HANGING BASKETS 3

❖

THERE are many more plants to consider: some are raised from seeds, others by cuttings. Plants raised from seeds are usually half-hardy annuals and are therefore discarded at the end of summer, but plants with a perennial nature, like small-leaved ivies, can be replanted in autumn into other containers.

RAISING PLANTS

• Cascade Geraniums: These are also known as Continental Geraniums and Swiss Balcon Geraniums, although botanically they are not geraniums but forms of pelargoniums. Many of the varieties are patented and are usually bought as established plants in mid to late spring, either from nurseries or through the mail from seed companies.

• Ivy-leaved Geranium *(Pelargonium peltatum):* Increased from cuttings, 6–7.5cm/2$\frac{1}{2}$–3in long, during late summer. Insert them in equal parts moist peat and sharp

sand, place in a cool greenhouse and cover their leaves with newspapers for about ten days. When rooted, pot up, place in 7–10°C/45–50°F and keep barely moist. Shelter from sunlight and remove the tips of shoots to encourage bushiness. Plant into containers as soon as the risk of frost has passed. During winter, keep the compost barely moist, as soft growth must be prevented.

VARIEGATED IVIES

The range of small-leaved, variegated ivies suitable for planting in hanging baskets is wide. And many of these can also be grown indoors. When grown in hanging baskets they are planted in spring. In late summer – when annual plants are removed – they can be put into winter displays in windowboxes, or troughs and tubs on patios.

CASCADE GERANIUMS *(Continental Geraniums): Height 20–30cm/8–12in, then trailing, plant 15–20cm/6–8in apart. Cascading, with masses of flowers in shades of scarlet, salmon, pink and lilac.*

PELARGONIUM PELTATUM *(Ivy-leaved Geraniums): Height 20–25cm/8–10cm, then cascading and trailing; plant one in a small hanging basket, or three in a large one. Summer flowering.*

GLECHOMA HEDERACEA *'Variegata' (Variegated Ground Ivy): Height 7.5–10cm/3–4in, then trailing, plant 25cm/10in apart. Mid-green, kidney-shaped leaves with white marks.*

HEDERA HELIX *(Small-leaved Ivy)*: Height 7.5–10cm/3–4in, then trailing, plant 15–16cm/5–6in apart. Select variegated varieties for planting around a basket's edge. In autumn, plant them in windowboxes.

HELICHRYSUM PETIOLATUM *(Licorice Plant)*: Height 15–20cm/6–8in, then cascading and spreading, plant 25cm/10in apart. Stiff stems peppered with roundish, white leaves covered with woolly hairs.

IMPATIENS *(Busy Lizzie)*: Height 15cm/6in, then cascading, plant 15–20cm/6–8in apart. Choose cascading varieties. Masses of flowers, up to 5cm/2in across, in many colours throughout summer.

• Variegated Ground Ivy (*Glechoma hederacea* 'Variegata'/ *Nepeta hederacea* 'Variegata'): It is easily increased by dividing plants in early spring. Discard old, central areas and replant younger pieces from around the outside.

• Small-leaved Ivy (*Hedera helix*): Take 6cm/2¹/₂in-long stem-and-leaf cuttings during summer and insert in equal parts moist peat and sharp sand. Place in gentle warmth and pot up when rooted.

• Licorice Plant (*Helichrysum petiolatum/H. petiolare*): During mid and late summer, take cuttings from sideshoots. Insert them in equal parts moist peat and sharp sand. Move rooted cuttings into small pots and overwinter in a cool greenhouse. Plant into hanging baskets during late spring.

• Busy Lizzie (*Impatiens*): Sow seeds 3–6mm/¹/₈–¹/₄in deep during mid-spring in 15–20°C/ 59–68°F. Germination takes ten to fourteen days. When large enough to handle, prick out the seedlings into seed-trays, acclimatize to outdoor conditions.

INTOXICATION AND FIDELITY

In earlier times, ivy was held in esteem and dedicated to Bacchus, the Roman god of wine, and widely used in crowns and wreaths. Historical writings suggest that the effects of intoxification were removed if a handful of bruised ivy leaves were gently boiled in wine and drunk.

Many centuries later, English taverns frequently bore a depiction of ivy over their doors to indicate the excellence of their beers and wines.

Ivy also had a loyalty factor. Greek priests presented wreaths of ivy to newly-married couples as an emblem of fidelity. Although early Christian thinking absorbed many pagan customs, the decoration of houses and churches with ivy was strictly forbidden.

PLANTS FOR
HANGING BASKETS 4

❖

HERE are more summer-flowering plants to choose from: many of those suggested here are raised each year from seeds.

RAISING PLANTS

• <u>Trailing Lobelia (*Lobelia erinus*)</u>: Sow seeds – barely covering them – from mid-winter to early spring in 15–20°C/59–68°F. Germination takes one to two weeks. When large enough to handle, prick out the seedlings into small clusters in a seed-tray. Then, slowly acclimatize the plants to outdoor temperatures.

• <u>Creeping Jenny/Moneywort</u> (*Lysimachia nummularia* 'Aurea'): It is easily increased by lifting and dividing established plants in spring. Use this yellow-leaved form instead of the normal type, as it is slightly less invasive and creates colour throughout summer. It also bears bright golden-yellow, cup-shaped flowers. It is ideal in large hanging baskets, as well as wall baskets and mangers.

• <u>Monkey Flower (*Mimulus* 'Malibu Orange')</u>: Sow seeds thinly – just pressing them into the surface of compost – during early summer in 16–20°C/61–68°F. Germination takes ten to fourteen days. When the seedlings are large enough to handle, transfer into seed-trays, then slowly accustom to outdoor conditions.

• <u>Nasturtium (*Tropaeolum majus*)</u>: Sow seeds 6mm/¼in deep in 13–16°C/55–61°F in late winter and early spring. Germination takes ten to fourteen days. When the seedlings are large enough to handle, move them into small pots. Do not grow them in rich compost, as they then develop too many shoots, at the expense of flower production.

• <u>*Nemophila maculata* '5-Spot'</u>: Sow seeds 6mm/¼in deep in 15°C/59°F in early spring. Germination

LOBELIA ERINUS
(Trailing Lobelia): Height 10–15cm/4–5in, then trailing, plant 10cm/4in apart. Select trailing varieties, in colours including blue, white, lilac and crimson. They flower throughout summer.

LYSIMACHIA
NUMMULARIA *'Aurea'*
(Moneywort/Creeping Jenny): Height 5–7.5cm/ 2–3in, then trailing, plant 20–25cm/8–10in apart. Hardy, herbaceous perennial with long stems, yellow leaves and golden flowers.

MIMULUS *'Malibu Orange' (Monkey Flower): Height 13–15cm/5–6in, plant 15cm/6in apart. Orange flowers during summer. Also, mixed-colour varieties – cream, golden-orange, red and burgundy – throughout summer.*

TROPAEOLUM MAJUS
'Double Gleam Mixed'
(Nasturtiums): Height
20–30cm/8–12in, then
trailing, plant 15–20cm/
6–8in apart. Semi-double,
scented flowers in yellow,
orange and scarlet. Also,
plant the 'Whirlybird'.

NEMOPHILA
MACULATA '5-Spot':
Height 7.5–15cm/3–6in,
then trailing: plant 20cm/
8in apart. Light green leaves
and beautiful light blue
flowers with a deep blue
spot at the tip of each petal.
It is ideal in light shade.

NEMOPHILA MENZIESII
'Pennie Black': Height
5–10cm/2–4in, then
spreading to about 30cm/
12in wide: plant 23cm/9in
apart. Purple to black
flowers, about 18mm/^{3}/$_4$in
wide with scalloped, white
edges – throughout summer.

takes ten to fourteen days. When
large enough to handle, transfer
the seedlings into small pots and
slowly acclimatize to outdoor conditions. Do not expose frost.

• _Nemophila menziesii_ 'Pennie
Black': Raise new plants each year
in the same way as recommended
for _Nemophila maculata_, a closely
related, bushy annual.

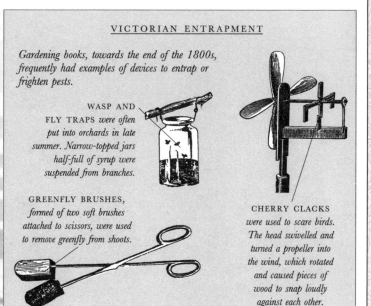

VICTORIAN ENTRAPMENT

Gardening books, towards the end of the 1800s,
frequently had examples of devices to entrap or
frighten pests.

WASP AND
FLY TRAPS were often
put into orchards in late
summer. Narrow-topped jars
half-full of syrup were
suspended from branches.

GREENFLY BRUSHES,
formed of two soft brushes
attached to scissors, were used
to remove greenfly from shoots.

CHERRY CLACKS
were used to scare birds.
The head swivelled and
turned a propeller into
the wind, which rotated
and caused pieces of
wood to snap loudly
against each other.

PLANTS FOR
HANGING BASKETS 5

❖

T HE ESSENTIAL
qualities of
plants for hanging
baskets are that they
should have a cas-
cading or trailing
nature, and create
a vivid display
throughout summer.
Those described
here will create a
feast of colour.

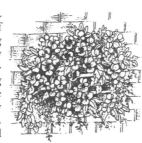

MOST *of the plants used
in hanging baskets are raised
from seeds sown early in the
year in gentle warmth, and later
transferred to pots or seed-trays.*

RAISING PLANTS
• *Nierembergia* 'Mont
Blanc': Sow seeds
3–6mm/^{1}/$_8$–^{1}/$_4$in
deep in 15°C/59°F in late winter
and early spring. When the
seedlings are large enough to handle, transfer them into seed-trays
and slowly acclimatize to outdoor
conditions and temperatures.
• Pansies (viola): Sow seeds
6mm/^{1}/$_4$in deep in 10–16°C/
50–61°F in late winter and early
spring. Germination takes two to

three weeks. When
large enough to han-
dle, prick out the
seedlings into small
pots and slowly accli-
matize to outdoor
conditions. Plant into
containers in early
summer.
• Garden Petunia
(*Petunia* x *hybrida*):
Sow seeds thinly on
the surface of com-
post during winter
and early spring in
15–20°C/59–68°F.
Germination takes
one to two weeks. When large
enough to handle, move the
seedlings into seed-trays and slowly acclimatize to outdoor conditions. Do not put the young plants
into containers until all risk of
frost has passed.
• *Silene pendula* 'Peach Blossom':
Sow seeds 3–6mm/^{1}/$_8$–^{1}/$_4$in deep
in 15°C/59°F in late winter or

NIEREMBERGIA *'Mont
Blanc': Height 10–15cm/
4–6in, plant 13–15cm/
5–6in apart. It creates a
mass of 2.5cm/1in-wide,
cup-shaped, white flowers
throughout summer. Remove
dead flowers regularly and
position in full sun.*

PANSY *'Water Colours
Mixed' (Viola): Height
10–15cm/4–6in, plant
10cm/4in apart. Weather-
resistant variety, ideal in
hanging baskets with flowers
in many delicate shades in
winter and spring, as well
as summer.*

PETUNIA *x* HYBRIDA
*(Garden Petunia): Height
10–15cm/4–6in, then
cascading, plant 20cm/8in
apart. Select cascading
varieties. Some are single
colours, other mixtures are
blue, white, pink, blush,
cerise, scarlet and violet.*

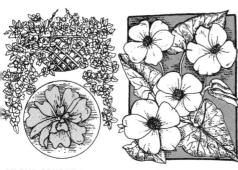

SILENE PENDULA
*'Peach Blossom': Height
10–15cm/4–6in, then
cascading, plant 20–25cm/
8–10in apart. Spreading
and branching, with masses
of 18mm/³/4in-wide,
double flowers. Deep pink
buds open to salmon and
mature to white.*

THUNBERGIA ALATA
*(Black-eyed susan): Height
90cm/3ft, but also trails
when in hanging baskets.
Thunbergia fragrans 'Angel
Wings', with snow-white,
lightly fragrant flowers, is
also good in hanging baskets
and pots. Creates a wealth
of colour in summer.*

VERBENA x HYBRIDA
*(Vervain): Height 23cm/
9in, then trailing, plant
15–25cm/6–10in apart.
Plant three in a hanging
basket. Select trailing
varieties, such as 'Peaches 'n
Cream', in beautiful shades
of cream, apricot, orange
and yellow.*

early spring. When large enough
to handle, transfer the seedlings
into seed-trays or small pots and
slowly acclimatize to outdoor conditions. Plant into containers as
soon as all risk of frost has passed.

• Black-eyed susan (*Thunbergia
alata*): Sow seeds 6mm/¹/4in deep
in 20°C/68°F during early and
mid-spring. Germination takes
about three weeks. When the
seedlings are large enough to handle, transfer them to small pots.
Slowly harden them off and plant
into containers on patios when all
risk of frost has passed.

• Vervain (*Verbena* x *hybrida*): Sow
seeds 3mm/¹/8in deep from late
winter to early spring in 15–
20°C/59–68°F. Germination takes
two to three weeks. When growing strongly, transfer the seedlings
into seed-trays. Harden off the
plants and transfer to containers
when all risk of frost has passed.

During recent years, new varieties have been developed in
North America and Britain, many
ideal for hanging baskets.

POPULAR VIOLETS

The Heart's-ease (Viola
tricolor) *was beloved by
Elizabethans and especially poets
and dramatists. William
Shakespeare (1564–1616)
clearly had an affection for them,
as in* A Midsummer Night's
Dream *he writes:*

*'I know a bank whereon the wild
thyme blows,
Where oxlips and the nodding
violet grows'*

*Its popularity is reinforced by its
wealth of names including Love-
in-idleness, Kiss-her-in-the-but-
tery, Three-faces-under-a-hood
and Cuddle-me.*

MIXING AND MATCHING PLANTS

 AS WELL as matching the colours of hanging baskets' flowers and leaves to their backgrounds, such as white, grey and red-bricked walls (pages 10 and 11), colour contrasts and harmonies within each basket are desirable. Also, there needs to be a variation in the shapes and sizes of plants within each basket.

SELECTING PLANTS

Apart from the colour theme or contrasts within a basket, when selecting plants consider the following points:

• Do not select more than three different types of plants for small baskets, or four when planting larger ones. If more than these are used, creating colour contrasts becomes difficult. It also can be confusing to the eye – and mind – which invariably likes to analyse and separate mixtures into their component parts.

• Select trailing plants that quickly clothe the basket's sides. There are many to choose from, in a wide range of colours. Many of these plants are traditional and have been used for years, such as trailing lobelia and alyssum, but a few more recent ones such as *Nierembergia* 'Mont Blanc' are worth trying.

• Unless the basket is packed with the same plants, such as petunias, Busy Lizzies or pansies, choose a dominant plant for the centre. This will give height and create a focal point. Cascading fuchsias are frequently used in these positions and can be selected so that their colours harmonize with the trailing plants at the outside. A range of fuchsia varieties for hanging baskets is detailed on pages 28 and 29.

• Foliage plants complete many trios and have the advantage of creating height and width without drenching the display in tightly

PLANT *hanging baskets with three or – at the most and only when the basket is large – four different types of plants. Here is a combination of flowering and foliage plants that creates interest throughout summer.*

SELECT *trailing forms of lobelia to cloak the basket's sides, with the attractively leaved* Helichrysum petiolatum *to introduce width to the display. The Ivy-leaved Geranium creates leaf-shape contrast.*

Ivy-leaved Geranium

Trailing lobelia

Helichrysum petiolatum

Trailing nasturiums

Dwarf marigolds

Dwarf marigolds

BASKETS *formed totally of flowering plants create vibrant colour displays that soon attract attention. Choose a selection of cascading, upright and bushy plants to ensure the basket becomes totally covered.*

THIS *basket is planted with nasturtiums, dwarf marigolds and trailing lobelia. Petunias can be substituted for the marigolds where a range of more subtle colours is desired, or to suit a different background.*

packed stems, flowers and leaves. For example, the gaps plants such as the Licorice Plant (*Helichrysum petiolatum*) create between their stems introduces light and air to a display and prevents it from appearing too solid. This is especially important in rural situations, where colour-dominant displays are less appealing than in towns. Foliage plants also help to perpetuate a display through to the frosts of autumn.

VARIEGATED TRAILERS

Several hardy variegated plants, such as ivies and Ground Ivy (*Glechoma hederacea* 'Variegata') are used to cloth the sides of baskets, but if too many are used, their colourful leaves can dominate the basket and immediate capture the eye at the expense of flowering plants. Therefore, use brightly coloured types sparingly, so that they create a framework for demure, but nevertheless attractive, flowers.

Glechoma hederacea 'Variegata' is often listed in catalogues as *Nepeta hederacea* 'Variegata'.

BRIGHTENING BALCONIES

Areas underneath balconies are usually bland and unappealing, but have several advantages: they create frost and rain-sheltered positions, with overhead projections that are ideal for supporting hanging baskets.

*In addition to hanging baskets, position tubs and urns underneath, so that the area can be colour co-ordinated. For example, vivid-red varieties of Basket Begonias (*Begonia x tuberhybrida* 'Pendula') growing in hanging baskets can be colour matched by the more upright forms of *Begonia x tuberhybrida* in pots and urns.*

Because balconies are visually dominant, balance them by using three hanging baskets, constrast the centre with the two outer ones.

MIXING AND
MATCHING PLANTS 2

❖

PLANTING schemes for flower borders in gardens are often a medley of colours, but some are formed of specific hues, such as white, grey, orange, green or blue. The same philosophy can be pursued for plants in hanging baskets, although it is best to restrict them to pastel shades, such as white and silver, and light blue. These create more relaxing ambiences on patios and terraces than if packed with vivid red flowers.

COLOUR-DEDICATED BASKETS

For white and silver baskets there are many plants to choose from, but avoid those with excessively white flowers as these will make the others look dowdy: they capture too much attention, especially when in bright sunshine. Use plenty of trailing plants, so that the display has well-covered irregular edges and appears to blend with its surroundings.

Combining them with silver-leaved or green-and-white variegated plants helps to reduce the impact of bright, white flowers.

Light blue designs have a warmer aura than white-and-silver ones and are superb when positioned against light grey, colour-washed walls. Unlike white-coloured arrangements, try to smother all the leaves with colour as green tends to dominate blue flowers, rather than complimenting them. Single-colour theme baskets bursting with light blue lobelia are especially attractive.

If there is an aged invalid in your house who is likely to sit outside during summer, use baskets planted with pastel-coloured plants, together with light green or silver-leaved foliage. Vivid reds and scarlets can soon disorientate people who are unwell, whereas restful-looking colours help to create an ambience that encourages speedy recovery.

CASCADING *petunias are superb plants for hanging baskets, especially in large containers where they can be collared with trailing plants, and peppered with a few marigolds to add a rich yellow sparkle.*

ALTERNATIVES *to petunias could be Busy Lizzies (in a wide colour range), while trailing forms of lobelia are in white, crimson, blue and lilac, so that almost any colour harmony can be created.*

Cascading petunias

Dwarf marigolds

Trailing lobelia

HANGING BASKETS

TRAILING *fuchsias
have informal outlines
that harmonize with Ivy-
leaved Geraniums. Select
trailing lobelia with
flower colours that
create rich colour
contrasts.*

NASTURTIUMS *are
also informal, with a
countrified, often lax
outline. Unfortunately,
they attract blackfly
and therefore frequent
spraying is usually
essential.*

Cascading fucshias

Trailing nasturtiums

Trailing lobelia

VICTORIAN EXPERIMENTATION

*Victorian gardeners had great
vitality and a desire to explore new
ways to use plants. Some of the
plants they grew outdoors in
suspended pots and other containers
were hardy and earlier grew in
borders and rock gardens.*

THE *Ice Plant*
(Mesembryanthemum
crystallinum), *prostrate, much-
branched, was grown in rock
gardens. It was also ideal for
planting in a suspended pot, where
its stems trailed up to 60cm/2ft.*

SIEBOLD'S *Stonecrop*
(Sedum sieboldii), *although
half-hardy, was grown in
rock gardens outdoors. When
planted in a hanging pot it
created a magnificent display.
Today, both this and a
variegated form (S. s.
'Medio-variegatum') are grown
in indoor hanging baskets.*

KNOWN *widely as Mother
of Thousands and Creeping
Sailor,* Saxifraga stolonifera
*is only half-hardy outdoors in
temperate areas. When planted
in ornate pots and used
outdoors in summer and
indoors in winter it became
very popular. The thin,
thread-like, wiry stems often
trail for several feet.*

SCENTED ARRANGEMENTS

❖

FRAGRANCES introduce a further quality to patios, making them more inviting in summer and creating a friendlier environment. Everyone – except those who have totally lost their sense of smell and are said to be anosmic – can, to varying degrees, detect and appreciate fragrances.

Young people are better able than the elderly to detect smells, although the ability still remains at a youthful level up to middle age and into retirement. And, surprisingly, people who work indoors are often better able to identify odours than those who continually work outdoors. Dark haired people are said to have a more sensitive appreciation of smell than those with fair hair.

EVENING AND NIGHT SCENTS

Flowers that saturate patios with rich fragrances at night are best grown in troughs or flower beds under windows. There are many plants to choose; a mixture of Night-scented Stocks and Virginian Stocks is superb.
• Night-scented Stocks: Sow seeds 6mm/¹/₂in deep from early to late spring, where they are to flower. Thin seedlings 15–23cm/ 6–9in apart.
• Virginian Stocks: Sow seeds 6mm/¹/₂in deep from early to late spring, where they are to flower. Thin the young seedlings to 15cm/6in apart. Plants flower about four weeks after being sown, and continue in flower for up to eight weeks.

CREATING A SCENTED PATIO
Do not just rely on scented plants in hanging baskets to create a fragrant patio. Use a combination of hanging baskets, tubs, pots, urns and troughs, as well as flower beds under windows. Also consider climbers planted in a bed and encouraged to clamber around windows. Many of these plants bear sweetly-scented flowers, but some have unusual fragrances, and these include:
• <u>Climbers:</u> wisteria (vanilla), *Clematis flammula* (hawthorn), *Jasminum officinale* (jasmine), *Lonicera* x *americana* and *L.* x *heckrottii* (honey), Rose 'Paul Transon' and Rose 'René André' '(apple-like), Rose 'Blush Noisette' (cloves), Rose 'Leander' (fruity), Rose 'Constance Spry' (myrrh) and Rose 'The Garland' (orange).
• <u>Tubs, pots and borders around patios:</u> *Nerium oleander* (almond), *Buxus sempervirens* 'Elegantissima' (honey), dwarf and slow-growing forms of *Juniperus communis* and *Thuja occidentalis* (apple), *Santolina chamaecyparissus* (chamomile), dwarf and slow-growing forms of *Thuja plicata* (pineapple), *Lilium candidum* (honey), *Lilium longiflorum* (Honey), dwarf and slow-growing forms of *Chamaecyparis lawsoniana* (resin and parsley), *Rosmarinus officinalis* (rosemary), *Salvia officinalis* (sage), dwarf and slow-growing forms of *Juniperus virginiana* (soap and paint), dwarf and slow-growing forms of *Chamaecyparis obtusa* (warm and sweet) and the dwarf and slow-growing forms of *Chamaecyparis pisifera* (resin).
• <u>Herbs in containers:</u> Further enrich the air with culinary herbs in pots, windowboxes and tubs. A few can be grown in wall and hanging baskets (see page 43).

WISTERIAS *create a wonderful display of vanilla-scented, pendulous clusters of violet-blue flowers during early summer. There is also a white-flowered form. It is superb when trained against a wall, and it can also be grown in a large tub.*

IN THE *centres of large baskets, plant three short, bushy, hybrid godetias (such as 'Satin Mixed') to produce a colour impact. Then, put several faintly but sweetly scented trailing nasturtiums around them. Their leaves, when crushed, are pungent.*

PLANT *a trailing fuchsia in the centre of a basket (see pages 28 and 29 for suitable varieties), with trailing Alyssum (Alyssum maritimum/Lobularia maritima) around the edges. These have the bouquet of new-mown hay and are attractive to bees.*

SMALL *conifers in tubs create colour throughout the year — and some have fragrant foliage when crushed.* Chamaecyparis lawsoniana 'Ellwood's Gold' *has a bouquet of resin and parsley.*

MANY *fragrant plants are ideal for growing in troughs or beds under windows or around the edges of patios and verandahs. The Night-scented Stock* (Matthiola bicornis) *drenches the air with rich sweetness during mid and late summer, while the Virginian Stock* (Malcolmia maritima) *also has sweetly scented flowers. Stocks have a bouquet like the scent of cloves.*

PANSIES *have a refreshing, cool, faintly sweet fragrance, but need to be grown* en masse *to create a detectable impact. Varieties with soft colours create a cooler and more refreshing ambience than those with strong tones. Choose varieties suitable for hanging baskets. Pansies are also ideal for growing in wall baskets. This allows a more dominant display to be created.*

ROSEMARY *is well known for its strongly aromatic leaves and mauve flowers, which although mainly appearing in spring usually continue sporadically until late summer or even into winter. Put five or seven plants in a large tub and keep nipping out their growing points to encourage bushiness. As well as creating a wonderful bouquet, Rosemary leaves are used in cooking.*

VEGETABLES AND FRUITS

HANGING baskets are not well known as containers for vegetables and fruits, and the reasons are clear: limited area for roots, risk of the compost drying out, inability for plants to be supported, and exposure to excessive temperatures and warm, drying winds. Wall baskets and mangers offer more congenial conditions.

However, seed companies have created varieties of tomatoes and strawberries specifically for growing in hanging baskets. Also, strawberries and tomatoes, as well as cucumbers and sweet peppers, are ideal for growing in wall baskets and mangers.

RAISING PLANTS

• <u>Tomatoes:</u> Sow seeds 3–6mm/ ⅛–¼in deep in early spring and place in 15–18°C/59–64°F. After germination, slightly lower the temperature and when the seed-

> ### GREEN PRECAUTIONS
>
> *To keep tomato plants free from whiteflies, grow a few marigolds nearby. Also, the annual herb Sweet Basil is said to be an insect repellent. Either buy plants or raise them from seeds sown in spring. Grow them in pots and position near to the tomatoes.*

lings have two pairs of true leaves transfer them into individual pots about 7.5cm/3in wide. Place them in gentle warmth, good light but not strong sunshine. Keep the compost moist but not continually saturated. Slowly acclimatize the plants to outdoor conditions and plant into containers as soon as all risk of frost has passed. Bush varieties remain low and there is no need to remove sideshoots.

GROWING *strawberries need not be left to gardeners with large gardens; the introduction of seed-raised varieties, such as 'Temptation', has made it possible to grow them successfully in hanging baskets. It fruits from mid-summer to the frosts of autumn. The fruits are richly aromatic.*

TOMATOES *in hanging baskets are possible, but choose a suitable variety. The bushy 'Tumbler' was specially developed for growing in baskets. It develops succulent, small, cherry-sized fruits. Plant it in large hanging baskets, using three plants, or plant one in a small basket.*

SWEET PEPPERS *are not ideal in hanging baskets, but can be grown in wall baskets and mangers. They grow 30–40cm/12–16in high and need a warm, sunny position and plenty of water. In large mangers use three plants, 30–38cm/12–15in apart.*

CUCUMBERS *can be grown in wall baskets: the compact 'Bush Champion' develops cucumbers for cutting within two months of being planted. It is ideal for containers on a patio: put two or three in a large manger, where they develop high quality, 25cm/10in-long cucumbers.*

• <u>Cucumbers:</u> Sow seeds singly and about 12mm/^{1}/$_2$in deep in small pots of peat-based compost in early or mid-spring. Place in 20–24°C/68–75°F. After germination, lower the temperature slightly. Keep the compost moist but not continually saturated and slowly acclimatize the plants to outdoor conditions. Plant them in containers as soon as all risk of frost has passed. Put three plants in a large manger, or one in a small wall basket.

• <u>Sweet Peppers:</u> Sow seeds 3–6mm/^{1}/$_8$–^{1}/$_4$in deep in early spring and place in 15–18°C/ 59–64°F. After germination, slightly lower the temperature and when the seedlings have four true leaves transfer them into individual pots, about 7.5cm/3in wide. Place them in gentle warmth and keep the compost moist. Slowly decrease the temperature and accustom them to outdoor conditions. After all risk of frost has passed, put three plants, about 30–38cm/12–15in apart, in a large manger.

• <u>Strawberries:</u> Traditionally, these have been increased by layering runners and encouraging them to form roots. Now, seed-raised plants are available.

HERBS IN HANGING BASKETS

Few herbs are diminutive enough for hanging baskets. However, trailing, perennial herbs such as thyme create attractive features – use variegated and golden-leaved forms. Even mint can, for novelty value, be put in a large hanging basket. Parsley is a better candidate and superb in a pot with holes in its sides, suspended against a white wall, where its green, attractively crinkled leaves create a colour contrast.

Wall baskets offer better places for herbs, but be prepared to plant them into herb gardens in autumn at the onset of cold weather.

PLANTS FOR
LOBBIES AND PORCHES 1

❖

THESE are half-way homes for houseplants, creating frost and rain-protected areas where some of the hardier types can be grown from late spring to early autumn.

Both flowering and foliage houseplants can be used, although to create interest throughout summer it is best to select those with coloured or variegated leaves. Nevertheless, Charm Chrysanthemums provide a spectacular display for several months.

PLANTING

There are two main ways of planting indoor hanging baskets for houseplants (see pages 18 and 19), and the same techniques can be used for plants in lobbies and porches. These involve either removing the pots and planting the soil-balls directly into compost, or leaving the pots in place and standing them in a group in a flat-bottomed, plastic hanging basket.

OTHER HOUSEPLANTS
TO CONSIDER

In addition to the trailing and cascading plants described here and on the following pages, there are several others which are suitable for hanging baskets in lobbies and porches, including:

• *Ficus pumila* 'Sonny' (Variegated Creeping Fig): This is similar to the normal, all-green Creeping Fig (page 46) but with white edges to small, green leaves. Put three plants in a small basket.

• *Coleus pumilus* 'Trailing Queen' (Trailing Coleus): Most coleus plants are upright and bushy, but this is a trailing type and ideal in summer in a lobby or porch. They are raised from seeds sown on the surface of compost in late winter or early spring and placed in 18–24°C/64–75°F. The seeds of other trailing varieties are widely available and include 'Moulten Lava' and 'Scarlet Poncho'.

• *Callisia elegans* (Striped Inch Plant): It is related and relatively

ASPARAGUS
DENSIFLORUS *'Meyeri'*
(Plume Asparagus/ Foxtail
Fern): Height 30–45cm/
12–18in, spread 30–
38cm/ 12–15in. Upright,
then arching, bottlebrush-like
stems with mid-green leaves.

ASPARAGUS
DENSIFLORUS *'Sprengeri'*
(Asparagus Fern/ Emerald
Fern/ Emerald Feather):
Height 25–30cm/ 10–12in,
spread 45–60cm/ 1¹/₂–
2ft. Arching, wiry stems
bearing mid-green leaves.

ASPLENIUM
BULBIFERUM (Mother
Fern/ Mother Spleenwort):
Height 38–45cm/ 15–18in,
spread 45–75cm/ 1¹/₂–
2¹/₂ft. Large, finely cut
fronds with small bulbils
that weigh them down.

CAMPANULA ISOPHYLLA *(Star of Bethlehem/ Italian Bellflower/ Falling Stars): Height 15cm/ 6in, spread 30–45cm/ 12–18in. Heart-shaped, mid-green leaves and star-shaped blue flowers in mid and late summer.*

CAREX MORROWII *'Variegata' (Japanese Sedge): Height 25–30cm/ 10–12in, spread 45– 60cm/ 1¹/₂–2ft. Arching, grass-like green leaves up to 30cm/ 12in long, with broad, creamy-white stripes. Very hardy.*

CHLOROPHYTUM COMOSUM *'Variegatum' (Spider Plant/ Ribbon Plant/ Spider Ivy): Height 15–25cm/ 5–10in, spread 60–90cm/ 2–3ft. Long, narrow leaves with white and green stripes. Plantlets on long stems.*

similar to the Wandering Jews (tradescantias) and develops fleshy, dull green leaves with white stripes and purple undersides. Plant it in a small pot, suspended or placed in a wall bracket.

• *Cyanotis kewensis* (Teddy Bear Vine): It is closely related to the tradescantias, but has densely hairy leaves, about 2.5cm/ 1in long. They are fleshy and their undersides are purple. For the best effect, display it on its own in a hanging pot.

• *Mikania ternata* (Plush Vine): A fast-growing, trailing plant for warm lobbies in summer. It makes a change from ivies, but is not as hardy and tolerant. The green, palmate leaves have an attractive purplish sheen.

• *Pellaea rotundifolia* (Button Fern/New Zealand Cliff Brake): Unusual fern, with small, button-like, leathery, dark green fronds on wiry stems. Do not mix it with other plants. Instead, plant it in a small pot and either suspend or place in a wall-bracket.

• *Peperomia scandens* 'Variegata' (Cupid Peperomia): It is often grown in a hanging basket indoors, and is equally at home in a warm lobby. Trailing stems bear succulent, somewhat heart-shaped, green leaves with broad yellow edges and patches.

VICTORIAN FERN LOVERS

During the Victorian era, ferns became very popular: many small ones were planted in Wardian Cases (enclosed glass cabinets evolved by Dr. Nathaniel Ward) as well as in borders and especially in damp situations. Forms of Phyllitis *scolopendrium with frilly edges were selected and formed ideal plants in cold, shaded conservatories.*

In 1866, one nursery offered eighty-two different types of this fern.

PLANTS FOR
LOBBIES AND PORCHES 2

❖

HERE are further houseplants that are sufficiently hardy to be displayed in lobbies and porches during summer. However, a few need warm positions, and this is indicated.

• *Cissus rhombifolia* 'Ellen Danica' (Mermaid Vine): Also known as *Rhoicissus rhomboidea* 'Ellen Danica', with leaves formed of deeply indentated, dark green leaflets. Grow on its own in a pot or hanging basket, where leaves can sprawl over the edges.

• *Sedum morganianum* (Donkey's Tail/Burro's Tail/Lamb's Tail): Succulent, with long stems clothed in cylindrical, grey-green leaves. Grow it in a pot on its own and position in a wall bracket in a warm lobby. Alternatively, place it in a suspended pot.

FASHIONABLE FEAST

As well as decorating homes and gardens with beautiful, brightly-coloured flowers, certain varieties of chrysanthemum in China have been grown for their edible petals, which are added to salads.

• *Selaginella uncinata* (Peacock Fern/Trailing Selaginella/Peacock Moss): Weak, trailing, straw-coloured stems bearing bluish-green leaves. Grow it on its own in a small pot and position in a wall bracket. The Mat Selaginella (*Selaginella kraussiana*) has bright green, slightly trailing stems, while 'Aurea' reveals yellow foliage.

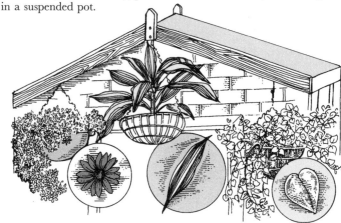

CHRYSANTHEMUM MORIFOLIUM – *Cascade Varieties: Height 10–15cm/ 4–6in, then trailing up to 38cm/15in or more. Masses of daisy-like flowers up to 4cm/1¹/₂in across, smothering the leaves in summer. Many varieties and colours.*

CORDYLINE TERMINALIS/C. fruticosa *(Ti Plant/ Flaming Dragon Tree): Height 38–45cm/15–18in, spread 30–38cm/12–15in. Tender and palm-like, with coloured leaves. Place in a warm lobby, with trailing plants positioned around it.*

FICUS PUMILA *(Creeping Fig): Height 5–7.5cm/2– 3in, then trailing. It is both a climbing and trailing plant, with small, somewhat heart-shaped leaves. It is best seen against a white background, or positioned around a central plant where it can trail.*

ICUS RADICANS
'*Variegata*' *(Trailing Fig):*
Height 7.5–13cm/3–5in,
then trailing. Cascading,
wiry stems, bearing lance-
shaped, slender-pointed, mid-
green leaves up to 6cm/
1/2in long with creamy
edges. Ideal in a basket on
its own.

LYSIMACHIA
NUMMULARIA '*Aurea*'
(Moneywort/Creeping
Jenny): Height 5–7.5cm/
2–3in, then trailing. Hardy
outdoor plant with trailing
stems, yellow leaves and
golden flowers. Ideal for
growing in cool and partly
open porches.

NEPHROLEPIS
EXALTATA *(Ladder*
Fern/Sword Fern): Height
30–38cm/12–15in, spread
50–60cm/20–24in – or
more. Upright and
cascading, deeply-divided,
sword-like fronds. N. e.
'*Bostoniensis*' *has more*
arching fronds.

Soleirolia soleirolii (Mind Your
Own Business/Baby's Tears/Irish
Moss): Earlier known as *Helxine
soleirolii*, this well-known Corsican
plant forms a mound of pale to
mid-green leaves clustered around
thin, trailing, pink stems. There
are several forms, such as

'Argentea' (leaves variegated in silver) and 'Aurea' (golden-green).
• _Stenotaphrum secundatum_ 'Variegatum' (Buffalo Grass/St.
Augustine-grass): Long, narrow,
green leaves, up to 13cm/5in
long, banded in white. The stems
often hang in irregular tufts.

FICUS PLANTS FOR LOBBIES AND PORCHES

The Rubber Plant (Ficus elastica) *is probably the best-known houseplant,
but there are many related species and some are hardy enough to be grown
in unheated lobbies and porches during summer.*
• *The Creeping Fig* (Ficus pumila) *is frequently grown
in hanging baskets and the ordinary, all-green type is
featured on page 46. There are also several
variegated forms, including* '*Sonny*' *with white
edges to the slightly crinkled leaves, and*
'*Variegata*' *with leaves marbled and lined in
cream and green.*
• *The Variegated Trailing Fig (*Ficus
radicans '*Variegata*') *is ideal (see above),
but position it in good light to encourage the
development of bright, rich colours in its spear-
shaped leaves.*

*Rubber plant
(*Ficus elastica)

PLANTS FOR
LOBBIES AND PORCHES 3

❖

 IN ADDITION to houseplants which are sufficiently hardy to be grown in porches and lobbies during summer, there are several hardy, trailing garden plants that are also ideal for these places.

INDOORS OR OUT?

The difference between a plant being hardy enough to be left outside in a garden or cosseted indoors is a matter of geography and micro-climates. Sometimes, only a matter of one hundred miles further south and a sheltered, sun-blessed position, turns a hardy houseplant into a garden type. For example, the Pig-a-back Plant (*Tolmiea menziesii*), although hardy enough to be planted outdoors in most areas, retains its foliage in better condition indoors or in a lobby (page 49).

The ordinary Creeping Jenny (*Lysimachia nummularia*) thrives well outdoors, but the yellow-leaved form 'Aurea' (page 47) retains its

colour and leaves better whe given protection from rain. Th Star of Bethlehem (*Campanula is phylla*) is frequently grown in hanging basket indoors, and i equally superb outdoors in sum mer or in a well-ventilated lobb or porch (page 44).

ANNUALS IN LOBBIES

Many of the plants suggested o pages 24 to 35, for planting i outdoor hanging baskets, can als be grown in lobbies and porche However, unless well ventilated lobbies can become too warm Porches are cooler. Also, wire framed hanging baskets will dri water over the floor. Therefore, it is the intention to suspend ther in lobbies or porches, use plasti baskets with drip trays fitted int their bases. And because of th increased temperatures they migh be exposed to in lobbies, ensur water-retaining additives (pages 1 and 15) are added to the compost

OPLISMENUS
HIRTELLUS *'Variegatus'*
*(Basket Vine): Height
5–7.5cm/2–3in, then
trailing. Creates a mass
of tumbling stems bearing
white-and-pink striped leaves
about 7.5cm/3in long. Ideal
in a hanging pot in a lobby.*

SAXIFRAGA
SARMENTOSA *'Tricolor'*
*(Mother of Thousands/
Strawberry Geranium):
Height 10–15cm/4–6in,
then trailing. This variety is
similar to the all-green type,
but with pink and pale
yellow variegations.*

SEDUM SIEBOLDII
'Medio-variegatum'
*(Variegated Siebold's
Stonecrop/Japanese Sedum):
Circular to heart-shaped,
green leaves with cream
blotches. Ideal in small pots
in warm lobbies; position
out of draughts.*

TOLMIEA MENZIESII
(Pig-a-back Plant/ Youth-on-age/ Thousand Mothers): Height 15cm/ 5in, then spreading and trailing. Large, long-stemmed, maple-like, mid-green leaves with plantlets peppered on their surfaces.

TRADESCANTIA FLUMINENSIS *'Variegata' (Wandering Jew): Height 5–7.5cm/ 2–3in, then trailing. Elliptic to oval leaves, about 5cm/ 2in long and striped in cream. There are many other varieties, some striped in silver.*

ZEBRINA PENDULA
(Silvery Inch Plant): Height 7.5–10cm/ 3–4in, then trailing. Thick stems bearing mid-green leaves with two silvery bands on their upper surfaces. Several varieties: 'Quadricolor' has green, silver, pink and red leaves.

MEMORIES AND MESSAGES

Memories are frequently evoked by flowers, although it is not usually necessary to garland oneself to the extent of this lady to capture thoughts of memorable moments. Bridal flowers are usually well recalled, as well as romantic strolls through gardens when often colour-rich flowers create the attraction. Some of these memories can be recaptured by planting these flowers in hanging baskets. Many flowers have messages that originated in the language of flowers, a method of communication 'without inking the fingers' that originated in Turkey in the 1600s. Each flower had a specific meaning and a few of them are relevant to plants that can be grown in hanging baskets:

- *African marigold = vulgar-minded*
- *Chrysanthemum (red) = I love*
- *Chrysanthemum (white) = truth*
- *Chrysanthemum (yellow) = slighted love*
- *Convolvulus = bonds/ uncertainty*
- *Fern = sincerity*
- *French marigold = jealousy*
- *Geranium = gentility*
- *Heart's-ease = you occupy my thoughts*
- *Lobelia = malevolence*
- *Stonecrop = tranquillity*
- *Strawberry = perfect excellence*
- *Thyme = activity*
- *Vervain = enchantment*

POCKET GARDENING GUIDES

ARRANGEMENTS FOR PORCHES AND LOBBIES

❖

USING porch and lobby plants in colourful and imaginative combinations is not expensive, but does need planning. Many lobby and porch plants are described on pages 44 to 49, and while some of them are ideal on their own, others are more gregarious. Together with a few others suggested here, these plants create outstanding displays.

COMBINATIONS TO CONSIDER

Several arrangements are illustrated here, but there are others to choose from, such as:

• Hanging baskets need not be packed with masses of different plants to create an interesting display. Indeed, such plant-packing techniques spoil the display. Instead, use a large fuchsia, with trailing nasturtiums around it. For a colour contrast, use a red-flowered trailing fuchsia and mixed or yellow nasturtiums.

• Flowering plants are not essential to hanging baskets. Indeed, an all-green arrangement can look exceedingly tasteful. Try a mixture of Asparagus Fern (*Asparagus densiflorus* 'Sprengeri') planted in the centre, surrounded by variegated ivies, Silvery Inch Plant (*Zebrina pendula*) and Variegated Sieboldi's Stonecrop (*Sedum sieboldii* 'Mediovariegatum'). This design is highlighted when positioned against a white wall.

• For a colour-packed hanging display, plant a pink-flowered *Begonia* 'Gloire de Lorraine' in the centre, with trailing, variegated ivies, cascading fuchsias and the trailing Basket Begonia (*Begonia × tuberhybrida* 'Pendula'). A variation on this is to substitute the silver-leaved *Helichrysum petiolatum* for the ivy. However, take care that the basket's width is not increased too much. The helichrysum has an advantage in that it is not as colour dominant as ivies.

A CENTRAL *Pouch Flower (calceolaria), trailing petunias and lobelia create a simple, inexpensive display. By using yellow and blue, the display is ideal for placing against a white wall in a cool lobby or porch.*

FOR *further interest, add a few trailing ivies, but not ones which are variegated in bright colours as they will dominate soft coloured lobelia. They could, however, be used with bright blue trailing lobelia.*

Cascading petunias

Trailing lobelia

Calceolarias

THIS *arrangement needs a warm lobby to ensure the dracaena in the centre remains healthy and grows. The Ivy-leaved Geranium and trailing lobelias introduce shape and colour contrasts.*

A VARIATION *on this hanging basket would be to use the tuberous-rooted and dominant Begonia x* tuberhybrida *instead of the dracaena. Select a variety with flowers that contrast with the others.*

Ivy-leaved Geranium

Dracaena

Trailing lobelia

SINGLE-PLANT THEMES

Many of the hardier houseplants that are suitable for porches and lobbies can be grown on their own in pots suspended by wires or decorative strings. Alternatively, plant them in pots placed in wall-brackets. These plants include:

- Basket Vine (*Oplismenus hirtellus* 'Variegatus') – page 48.
- Buffalo Grass (*Stenotaphrum secundatum* 'Variegatum') – page 47.
- Button Fern (*Pellaea rotundifolia*)– page 45.
- Donkey's Tail (*Sedum morganianum*) – page 46.
- Ladder Fern (*Nephrolepis exaltata*) – page 47.
- Mind Your Own Business (*Soleirolia soleirolii*) – page 47.
- Mother Fern (*Asplenium bulbiferum*) – page 44.
- Peacock Fern (*Selaginella uncinata*) – page 46.
- Pig-a-back Plant (*Tolmiea menziesii*) – page 49.
- Plume Asparagus (*Asparagus densiflorus* 'Meyeri') – page 44.
- Plush Vine (*Mikania ternata*) – page 45.
- Silvery Inch Plant (*Zebrina pendula*) – page 49.
- Spider Plant (*Chlorophytum comosum* 'Variegatum') – page 45.
- Striped Inch Plant (*Callisia elegans*) – page 44.
- Teddy Bear Plant (*Cyanotis kewensis*) – page 45.
- Trailing Fig (*Ficus radicans* 'Variegata') – page 47.
- Variegated Creeping Fig (*Ficus pumila* 'Sonny') – page 44.

INGENIOUS VICTORIANS

Several garden tools were invented or modified by the Victorians. The Reverend Huthwaite invented the Desideratum Watering Can to enable plants on high shelves to be watered. It was formed of a 1.5m/5ft-long bamboo cane with a forked, metal top from which was suspended a watering-can. When a string was pulled the can tilted and water trickled out.

PLANTING WALL
BASKETS AND MANGERS

THE TECHNIQUE of planting a wall basket or manger is similar to that used for wire-framed hanging baskets. However, it is usually easier because the basket is held firmly and often at waist height.

PREPARING AND PLANTING

It is essential to line the basket with polythene to prevent dirty, compost-soaked water running down walls and marking them. Use black polythene, as this is less conspicuous than white, although eventually it becomes clothed in trailing flowers, stems and leaves.

When piercing holes in the polythene at the basket's front, make them quite low down so that excess water can readily escape. Small wall baskets are especially susceptible to compost drying, so add moisture-retentive additives (see page 14).

Mangers and large wall baskets hold more compost and therefore have a greater reserve of moisture.

Firm the compost – but not excessively – to ensure it retains the maximum amount of moisture. After the plants have been set in position and compost firmed around their roots, the surface must be 18–25mm/$3/4$–1in below the basket's rim. During the following few weeks, the surface will settle slightly. Ensure that when the compost is watered it is possible to soak it thoroughly. If only a small space is left, it is difficult to soak the compost as water runs straight off the surface.

When planting wire-framed hanging baskets it is essential to put plants into their sides, but with wall baskets and mangers this is not necessary as they are displayed lower down and plants soon smother the edges. Nevertheless, if the sides of large mangers present large, bland areas, make slits near the top and put plants in them. Any of the trailing plants recommended for outdoor hanging baskets can be used to cover the sides.

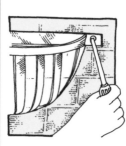

HOLD *a wall basket or manger in position and mark the positions of the securing holes. Drill the wall, insert masonry fixings and use galvanized screws to secure the basket to the wall.*

LINE *the inside with strong, black polythene, or two layers of large bin-liners. Ensure the back is covered to prevent water getting on the wall. Mould the liner to the basket's shape.*

FILL *the basket about half full with peat-based compost. Then, pierce holes in the polythene, but only at the front. This is to ensure that excess water escapes at the basket's front, not the back.*

CONTAINER COMBINATIONS

Wall baskets and mangers are displayed on their own on patios, usually leaves a space at ground level that, unless filled, looks bland and unplanned. However, when wall baskets are positioned on walls at the fronts of mews cottages, this can be as asset as the area underneath can be easily cleaned. When tubs are used in such positions, this task is difficult. However, here are a few ideas to create unified displays.

Use a combination of a large wall basket and a tub on either side of it to create an attractive feature against a long wall. Put trailing plants with long, cascading stems – such as the Variegated Ground Ivy – at the sides of the basket so that the display appears unified. And in each tub plant a tall, bushy plant – perhaps a standard fuchsia – to extend its lines upwards.

At the fronts of houses and where flower borders are under windows, a windowbox under the window and a wall basket on either side creates an attractive feature. It also can be colour co-ordinated with border flowers.

• Small wall baskets are ideal at the sides of front doors. For extra interest they can be positioned one above another, but beware of water dripping on to the lower one. Bright-faced Pansies look good in these positions, and do not encroach much on surrounding space.

• Wall baskets offer excellent opportunities for disabled people to garden. Try putting several of them on walls, with large tubs positioned between them.

TOP *up the basket with peat-based compost and firm it to within 7.5cm/3in of the top. If the basket is small, mix in additives such as perlite and vermiculite to assist in the water retention.*

START *planting the basket from the back, putting in bushy plants that will give height to the display. When planted, the compost's surface should be 18–25cm/3/4– 1in below the rim.*

FINALLY, *add trailing plants around the rim. Water them thoroughly to settle compost around their roots. These trailing plants will soon cloak the polythene and create a sheet of colour.*

CONTRASTS AND HARMONIES

❖

BACKGROUND colours behind wall baskets dramatically affect the attractiveness of a display. Here are examples of arrangements to suit a range of differently coloured backdrops.

Some flower colours can b used against several background This especially applies to whit which contrasts well with dark an red walls. Yellow plants also hav this useful, dual role

WHITE WALLS, *although bright, are uninteresting unless enriched with other colours, such as yellow, gold, scarlet or green. Above is a combination of zinnias, geraniums (pelargoniums), marigolds and the Emerald Fern* (Asparagus densiflorus 'Sprengeri').

ANOTHER *arrangement to suit a white wall is a cascading and trailing Emerald Fern* (Asparagus densiflorus 'Sprengeri'), *bright yellow calceolarias, several red-flowered trailing nasturtiums* (Tropaeolum majus) *and Iceland Poppies* (Papaver nudicaule).

GREY STONE WALLS *present a soft, relaxing background that is ideal for pink, red, deep purple and deep blue flowers. Above is a mixture of petunias, geraniums (pelargoniums) and the blue-flowered Star of Bethlehem* (Campunala isophylla), *a native of northern Italy.*

A FURTHER *arrangement for grey stone walls is cascading red or pink fuchsias (see pages 28 and 29 for suitable varieties), trailing begonias and an edging of silver-leaved plants such as the trailing and cascading Licorice Plant* (Helichrysum petiolatum).

RED BRICK WALLS *are strongly coloured and require bold splashes of soft blue, white or lemon flowers, as well as silver foliage. Above is an arrangement formed of white Marguerites* (Chrysanthemum frutescens), *soft blue trailing lobelia and blue stocks.*

ANOTHER *arrangement for a red-brick backdrop includes short-stemmed white tulips, deep blue-flowered Grape Hyacinths* (Muscari armeniacum) *and small-leaved, variegated ivies. This is an ideal arrangement for a spring to early summer display.*

DARK WALLS *can be both intimidating and dramatic. It is essential to use bright flowers as well as foliage plants with light or silver leaves. This basket is formed solely of Cinerarias.*

A MEDLEY *to suit dark backgrounds is the yellow-leaved Creeping Jenny* (Lysimachia nummularia 'Aurea'), *yellow caleolarias and the dominantly flowered tuberous-rooted begonias* (Begonia x tuberhybida).

INFLUENCE OF LIGHT

The perception of colour continually alters throughout the day, depending on the intensity of light. For example, bright sunshine glaring down at midday highlights yellow, gold and white more then red. And with the onset of evening, light colours remain more noticeable than dark shades. At that time, red and brown become almost black. For this reason, position containers with light-coloured plants near entrances.

UNUSUAL CONTAINERS

PATIOS, as well as lobbies and porches, are soon enriched by a few unusual pots or hanging baskets. Many garden centres specialize in these containers. Also, have a look in granny's attic for old bird cages or baskets.

When using old wickerwork baskets, first line them with plastic, but instead of planting directly into them, leave the plants in their pots and stand them in plastic saucers. In this way, the plants can be changed and the basket is not ruined through being continually soaked in water.

Always use plants that harmonize with the container. For example, bright-faced flowers will compete with wall pots that depict noble Greek faces. Instead, use trailing thyme or ivies – but avoid using brightly variegated types.

In bird cages, use climbing or trailing plants, so that their sides are clothed and softened.

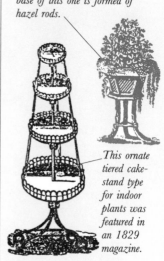

INDOOR DISPLAYS

Early Victorian plant containers could be extremely ornate. The base of this one is formed of hazel rods.

This ornate tiered cake-stand type for indoor plants was featured in an 1829 magazine.

MACRAMÉ *and other string-woven pot supports are ideal in lobbies, porches and conservatories. Even ordinary wickerwork baskets, planted with summer flowers, look good when suspended from ornate brackets.*

TERRACOTTA CONTAINERS
resembling faces seldom fail to attract
attention when secured to walls.
They look good when planted with
ivies, the yellow-leaved Creeping Jenny
(Lysimachia nummularia 'Aurea')
and thyme. When choosing plants to
feature in 'faced' containers, ensure
that they harmonize with the faces and
do not hide them. Ideally, position and
train the plants to create an attractive
frame. Sometimes they can simulate hair.

ORNATE BIRD CAGES *create*
dramatic homes for plants and are
particularly suited for displays in
large lobbies and conservatories.
Wall-mounted pots enable walls to
be peppered with colour, while slatted
baskets have a more clinical outline
than wire-mesh baskets. Novelty
containers, where excess water appears
like tears out of eyes, almost always
create amusement and interest.

PESTS AND DISEASES

MEALY BUGS *resemble small woodlice, but are covered with white, cotton-like fluff. Not an outdoor pest, but are occasionally seen on houseplants in lobbies. Spray with a systematic insecticide.*

CATERPILLARS *sometimes occur on plants in hanging and wall baskets. They chew leaves and flowers. Pick off and destroy these pests, and regularly spray with derris.*

GREENFLIES *(Aphids) suck sap and cause the general debilitation of plants. Spray regularly with suitable insecticide.*

WOODLICE *do not normally infest hanging baskets, but sometimes climb walls and chew plants in wall baskets. Dust with gamma-HCH.*

SLUGS *sometimes scale walls and infest wall baskets. Pick off and use slug baits.*

POWDERY MILDEW *sometimes coats leaves with a white powdery deposit. Occasionally seen on plants indoors, so check hanging baskets in lobbies. Pick off infected leaves, improve ventilation and spray with a fungicide.*

CYCLAMEN MITES *are sometimes seen on cyclamen and pelargoniums indoors. Therefore, check pelargoniums in hanging baskets in lobbies. Pick off infected leaves or destroy severely infested plants.*

EARWIGS *frequently infest plants in wall baskets. They chew petals and soft leaves, tearing them apart. Pick off and destroy them, and spray with malathion.*

WHITEFLIES *are like small, white moths and cluster on house-plants. They suck sap, causing mottling. Spray regularly, as they are difficult to control.*

PREVENTATIVE TREATMENT

Check flowers and leaves at least once a week and, if any of these plant problems are seen, spray them immediately; repeat the treatment as necessary.

THRIPS *infest plants indoors, in lobbies and outdoors, causing streaking and mottling. Spray with malathion or derris.*

RED SPIDERS *sometimes infest plants in lobbies. They suck sap, causing bleached areas. Increase ventilation, mist-spray leaves and spray with a systematic insecticide.*

SNAILS *sometimes climb walls and attack plants in wall baskets. Pick off and destroy and use baits.*

GREY MOULD *(Botrytis) creates fluffy, mouldy growths on flowers and soft stems. Cut off and destroy infected parts. Increase ventilation and spray with a fungicide.*

VIRUSES *stunt plants and create light-coloured patches on leaves and flowers. Destroy badly infested plants.*

HANGING BASKET CALENDAR

❖

SPRING

This is a busy season, although the degree of activity depends on the weather and if it is warm enough to plant hanging baskets in mid-spring. Where there is a risk of frost, either leave planting until early summer, or plant in mid-spring and place the basket in a greenhouse or conservatory until it is safe to put it outside.

- When buying plants, inspect them carefully (12–13).
- Before putting a hanging basket outdoors, ensure the bracket is strong and well secured to a wall (20).
- Where a greenhouse or conservatory is available for putting newly-planted hanging baskets into until they are established, plant hanging baskets in early to mid-spring (16–17).
- After planting a hanging basket, water it carefully (16–17).
- Remove the tips of shoots from plants such as fuchsias to encourage bushiness (16).
- Plant indoor hanging baskets in early spring. Although this can be done throughout the year, spring or early summer are the best times (18–19).
- Position houseplants (still in their pots) in indoor hanging baskets which have drip trays 18–19). As plants stop flowering or become unattractive, they can be replaced with others that are starting to flower.
- In warm areas, where hanging baskets can be placed outside in late spring, water them carefully and regularly (21).
- Select plants for lobbies and porches (44–49).
- Select plants for outdoor hanging baskets (24–35).

SUMMER

In cold areas it is best to wait until early summer before placing hanging baskets outdoors. Once outside, regularly listen to weather forecasts and cover the plants with a couple of layers of newspaper when frost threatens.

Plants in wall baskets are just as vulnerable, especially as these cannot first be placed in a greenhouse or conservatory to become established before being put outside.

- In early summer, continue to remove the tips of shoots from plants such as fuchsias to encourage bushiness (16).
- Position houseplants (still in their pots) in indoor hanging baskets with drip-trays (18–19). As plants stop flowering or become unattractive, they can be replaced.
- Water hanging baskets carefully and regularly throughout summer (21).
- On very hot days, place ice-cubes on the compost to give the plants an extra amount of water (21).
- If the compost becomes very dry, take down the basket and plunge it in water (21).
- Feed plants regularly during summer (22–23).
- Remove dead flowers and leaves throughout summer to keep the display tidy and to encourage the development of further flowers (22–23).
- Inspect plants regularly throughout summer to ensure they are not infested with pests or diseases (22–23 and 58–59).
- Although slugs and snails do not infest hanging baskets, they often climb into wall baskets. Put down baits (22–23). Place them under propped up files.

AUTUMN

Outdoors, displays in hanging baskets will be coming to an end, especially in areas where frosts arrive early. At the first risk of frost, put tender perennial plants, such as fuchsias and geraniums, in frost-proof greenhouses. Summer-flowering bedding plants, however, are just left to die.

Once the display is over, remove the baskets and place the plants on a compost heap. The compost in the basket is either dug into a vegetable garden or scattered on border soil.

Ensure all old compost is removed, then thoroughly wash baskets in hot water and disinfectant. Rinse the baskets to remove all traces of disinfectant.

Check brackets and chains, making a note to replace them in late winter or spring.

Clear out wall baskets and mangers and scrub and disinfect them. If they are looking old, take them down. Rub down the metalwork with sandpaper and repaint in readiness for the following year.

Also, take down clay pots suspended from wires, as well as those in wall-brackets. Again, clean and store them.

Many nurseries specialize in hanging baskets, selling plants as well as baskets ready-planted in spring and early summer. They usually take orders for baskets, so find out when the last order date is, so that you will not be disappointed in the spring.

Also, many seed catalogues specialize in seeds for hanging basket plants: order your catalogue and seeds now.

- Position houseplants (still in their pots) in indoor hanging baskets with drip trays (18–19). As plants stop flowering or become unattractive, they can be replaced.

WINTER

During winter, spring and early-summer may appear a long way off, but now is the time to plan the positions for hanging baskets and wall baskets, as well as the plants to go in them. Positioning and design factors are discussed on pages 8–9 and 53.

If watering hanging baskets was a problem during the previous year, consider buying a special watering lance that attaches to a hosepipe. Alternatively, tie a cane to the hosepipe. Another method is to have a pulley, so that the basket can be lowered. Watering is certainly a prime task during summer, and can be difficult when standing on a chair or stool.

Each year, many superb hanging baskets are ruined while you are away on holiday during the peak summer months – and solely because a plant-sitter failed to water them adequately. Make watering an easier task for them during the coming year.

- In early and mid-winter, plan hanging baskets and order seeds of half-hardy bedding plants. Colour co-ordinate them with their backgrounds, as well as with each other (10–11).
- In early and mid-winter, plan the design of plants in wall baskets and mangers (54–55).
- In late winter, ensure baskets, liners and compost are ready (14–15).
- Position houseplants (still in their pots) in indoor hanging baskets with drip trays (18–19). As plants stop flowering or become unattractive, they can be replaced.
- In late winter, check that brackets supporting hanging baskets are still secure. If not, remove and replace them (20). Pull and push them several times as a final check.

USEFUL HANGING
BASKET TERMS

❖

APHIDS: *Another name for greenflies. Also, sometimes known as aphis. They suck the sap of soft-stemmed plants, causing debilitation as well as spreading viruses from one plant to another.*

BARGE-BOARD: *The overhanging wooden board (now frequently formed of a plastic material) along the projecting sloping edge of a gable roof. Hooks can be screwed into those formed of wood, and used to suspend hanging baskets.*

BLACKFLY: *A type of aphid. They frequently become pests of soft-stemmed plants, congregating around leaves, stems and flowers and slowly destroying them.*

CASCADING: *A gentle sweeping downwards, as opposed to trailing when plant stems tumble vertically.*

CENTRE-PIECES: *Plants put in the centres of containers to create dominant displays. In hanging baskets, fuchsias are frequently planted for this purpose.*

COIR-BASED COMPOST: *A type of compost that does not include peat and therefore is termed environmentally friendly.*

COMPOST ADDITIVES: *Materials added to composts to enable them to retain extra moisture – see perlite and vermiculite.*

CORK: *A material used to retain moisture in containers in Victorian times. It was chopped up and added to composts, but has now been replaced by other materials.*

DAMPING OFF: *A fungal disease of seedlings in greenhouses. They collapse at compost level and do not recover. Compacted compost, high temperatures and congested seedlings help to initiate an attack. Attacks can be controlled by spraying with chemicals, but once seedlings collapse they never recover. This disease does not affect hanging baskets unless you raised your own plants.*

DRIP TRAY: *Integral with plastic-type hanging baskets to prevent water dripping on floors or plants beneath them. This type of hanging basket is frequently used in lobbies and porches, as well as indoors.*

FACE SIDE: *This is the side of plants that is most attractive.*

FOAM LINER: *Used to help retain moisture in hanging baskets.*

FROST-TENDER: *Plants that are killed or seriously damaged by exposure to frost. Such plants include half-hardy summer-flowering annuals, and tender perennials.*

FUNGICIDE: *A substance for killing fungal diseases.*

HALF-HARDY ANNUALS: *Tender annuals, raised in gentle warmth in late winter or early spring, slowly acclimatized to outdoor conditions and planted into containers or borders outdoors when all risk of frost has passed.*

HANGING BASKET WATERER: *In addition to* home-made devices to help makewatering hanging baskets easier, proprietary types of waterersare available.

HANGING BASKET LINER: *Range of materials used to prevent compost falling through the holes in wire-framed baskets, as well as assisting in the retention of moisture.*

HANGING POT: *Clay-type pot that is suspended by wires and used to grow small, trailing plants.*

HARDEN OFF: *Acclimatizing plants to outdoor conditions. Especially associated with half-hardy summer-flowering bedding plants in spring.*

HARMONIZING: *Creating colour-pleasing combinations of plants with their backgrounds.*

HAYRACK: *Often sold for use as a plant container. Can be treated in exactly the same way as wall baskets and mangers.*

ICE CUBES: *Occasionally placed on top of compost in hanging baskets in summer to create additional, slowly available moisture.*

INDOOR HANGING BASKET: *Invariably made of plastic. One type is formed of a plastic-type bowl (with no drainage holes), another with a drip-tray fitted into its base. Plants are either removed from their pots and planted into compost, or left in their pots and just placed in the container (see pages 18 and 19).*

INSECTICIDE: *A substance for killing insects.*

LINER: *Used to prevent compost falling out of wire-framed baskets, as well as to assist in the retention of moisture in the compost.*

LOAM-BASED COMPOST: *Compost formed of a mixture of loam (good quality topsoil), peat and sharp sand. They do not retain as much moisture as peat-based types. However, they are widely used in tubs and pots on patios.*

LOBBY: *An enclosed area immediately outside a main door and with a separate door to the outside. Such areas are not usually heated, and create half-way positions between the house and garden.*

MACRAMÉ HOLDER: *Cords knotted and threaded into ornamental patterns to create harnesses for pots, so that they can be suspended.*

MANGER: *Similar to wire-framed wall baskets, but with metal bars instead of a wire frame.*

MASONRY FIXINGS: *Special wall fixings, inserted into holes drilled in walls. Screws can then be screwed into them to secure a wall basket or other feature.*

MIXING AND MATCHING: *Arranging plants so that they complement each other and form an attractive feature.*

NIPPING OUT: *Removing the growing tip of a shoot to encourage the development of sideshoots.*

PEA-SHINGLE: *Shingle, each piece about 6mm/¹/₄in in width.*

PEAT-BASED COMPOST: *Compost formed of peat. It retains more moisture than a loam-based type and is mainly suited for use in mangers, wall and hanging baskets.*

PERLITE: *A moisture-retentive material added to composts to increase their ability to retain moisture.*

PINCHING OUT: *Removing the growing tips of plants to encourage the development of sideshoots.*

PLASTIC LINER: *Black polythene is frequently used to create an inexpensive liner for hanging baskets, wall baskets and mangers.*

PORCH: *A covered area around a front or back door, open on one side but creating a rain and wind-sheltered area for plants. Such places are much cooler than lobbies.*

PRICKING OFF: *Transferring seedlings from where they were sown into seed-trays or pots. This gives them extra space in which to develop and grow. If left, the seedlings become thin and eventually collapse.*

PRICKING OUT: *Has a similar meaning as PRICKING OFF.*

SLOW-ACTING FERTILIZER: *Frequently added to compost in hanging baskets and other containers to ensure that plants have an adequate supply of food over a long period.*

SPACING: *Plants in containers are planted closer together than when in borders in gardens. And plants in hanging baskets are especially positioned closely so that they quickly create colourful, eye-catching displays.*

SPHAGNUM MOSS: *A type of moss, earlier and widely used to line wire-framed hanging baskets to prevent compost escaping and to retain moisture. Nowadays, it has been replaced by plastic sheeting and other liners, but is still often used to cover the surface of compost in hanging baskets to create an attractive finish.*

STOPPING: *Nipping out the growing point of a shoot to encourage bushiness.*

TENDER PERENNIALS: *Some plants grown in hanging baskets and wall baskets are not fully hardy and therefore cannot be put outside until all risk of frost has passed. Geraniums and fuchsias are examples of these plants.*

TRAILING: *Plants with stems that hang down almost vertically.*

VERMICULITE: *A moisture-retentive material added to compost to assist in water retention.*

WALL BASKET: *Similar in shape to a hanging basket cut in half. It is then secured to a wall and used to grow bushy and trailing plants.*

WALL BASKET LINER: *Proprietary material shaped like the inside of a wall basket and used to retain compost and assist in the retention of water.*

WALL BRACKET: *Metal bracket from which hanging baskets are suspended. They are available in several sizes.*

WIRE-FRAMED BASKET: *Hanging basket formed of wires, as opposed to plastic types that have solid sides and bases.*

INDEX
❖